THE
FALKNERS
OF MISSISSIPPI

THE
FALKNERS
OF MISSISSIPPI

a memoir

MURRY C. FALKNER

LOUISIANA STATE UNIVERSITY PRESS BATON ROUGE

To my wife Suzanne,
with love

FOREWORD

Yoknapatawpha and the World of Murry Falkner

by Lewis P. Simpson

MURRY FALKNER'S MEMOIR IS IMPORTANT FOR THESE, among other, reasons: it is a basic source for the study of the life and writings of a major American writer, his brother, William Faulkner; and it is an imaginative repossession of significant facets of American life in the first half of the twentieth century. The central inspiration of the book is the telling of the story of the Falkner brothers—how four Deep South boys grew up in a "closely knit and self-sustaining" family in the little community of Oxford, Mississippi, and then inevitably went their own ways, "each . . . to do what he had the capability to do and to refrain from doing what he had the capacity to withstand." In the remembering mind—affectionate, nostalgic, ironic—of the surviving brother, the three brothers who have gone the farther way into death, together with other members of the Falkner family, are reunited. Although Murry Falkner (known to his family as "Jack") is not a professional writer like his brothers William and John, he may well share with them a natural vocation.

Their great-grandfather, Colonel William C. Falkner, was a gifted amateur author who in 1881 published a novel called *The White Rose of Memphis*, a best seller for a whole generation. Perhaps when Murry Falkner began to write out of a sense of duty to William's memory, he was responding to a calling as well as an obligation.

As a source for the study of William Faulkner, *The Falkners of Mississippi* will disappoint the merely curious. They will find in it no revelations of great note about him or his family and scarcely any new information. But discerning students of Faulkner will, I believe, find this memoir quite fundamental to their inquiries into Faulkner's great artistic construct, the literary world of Yoknapatawpha County; for Murry Falkner has created out of his search into the past a world that sharpens our understanding of Yoknapatawpha.

What I mean has a great deal to do with Murry Falkner's style. In places it is purely genteel: "How kind they were, those years of long ago; how gentle the life and how pleasant the memories of it." More often *The Falkners of Mississippi* is written in a style resulting from a mixture of the genteel and the colloquial. One short passage will serve for illustration: "We were of a common conviction that had Auntee lived at the time of the War, the South would never (could never) have lost it, seeing that the Yankees had us outnumbered by only three or four to one. Surely Auntee would have made up this trifling difference without half trying. Ten or twelve to one would have put some strain on her, but anything less would have been unworthy of serious thought to one of her temperament and loyalty." This is the voice of Mark Twain, yet the writer is by no means deliberately imitating Mark Twain. He is choosing and ordering words according to a sense of expression that is genuinely American. It derives from the conflict in Murry Falkner's generation between the

"proper" or "literary" use of English and the insistence in
American informal language habits on the colloquial and the
vernacular. Under the conditions of democracy in America
this opposition of styles, which was stronger in rural than
urban areas, resulted in a kind of compromise, particularly
in written English. The compromise created a style that may
be taken in the largest signification of style—that is, a way of
thinking and feeling in words that gives life in a certain age
and place a distinctive voice. The state of literary consciousness in the small Southern community of the Falkner brothers'
boyhood and young manhood—the quality of the native literary environment—is illuminated by Murry Falkner's style.
Thus, *The Falkners of Mississippi* indicates a primary source
of the complex style, the complex of voices, through which
Yoknapatawpha comes into its intricate, multi-dimensional
existence.

There is a noticeable difference, it may be observed, between the styles of this memoir and the one by John Faulkner
entitled *My Brother Bill: An Affectionate Reminiscence* (published in 1963). Deceptively simple, written in a carefully controlled colloquial style, that work is the achievement of the
discipline of a literary artist who, like Hemingway, would not
have wanted to be caught dead with a genteel phrase in his
typewriter. Another distinction between *The Falkners of
Mississippi* and *My Brother Bill*, a matter of style in the largest
sense, bears more obviously on the implications of Murry
Falkner's book for the student of Yoknapatawpha. This is his
freedom from what may be termed without much exaggera-
tion the tyranny of Yoknapatawpha. I refer to the power of
the fictional world of Yoknapatawpha, one of the most convincing illusory worlds ever developed by a writer, to impose
itself on anything written about Oxford and Lafayette County,
Mississippi. Sitting on the steps of a funeral home in Oxford

waiting for his brother Bill's body to be brought there from
the hospital, John Faulkner looked out over the town square
and saw not only Bill and Jack (Murry) and himself but also
Will Green and Joe Christmas and Percy Grimm. "Everywhere I looked there was Bill and his stories: Oxford, Jeffer-
son, and Lafayette County, Yoknapatawpha." Murry Falkner
has apparently never fallen under this common spell. Nowhere in *The Falkners of Mississippi* do the people of William
Faulkner's mythic community appear to distort or shape the
author's remembrance. This is a great advantage. We seem
to be seeing the Falkners and their world in, so to speak, pre-
Yoknapatawpha times.

We have sketches of the Old Colonel and the Young
Colonel without the shadowing of the elegant doom of the
Sartorises. Most notably, we have unforgettable recollections
of Mammy Callie Barr which are uninfluenced by the powerful figure of Dilsey, the old Negro goddess of wisdom in *The
Sound and the Fury* who in the midst of the terrible degenera-
tion of the Compsons is faithful and enduring. Mammy Callie,
who had her own rocking chair by the Falkner fireplace and
was "an honored member of the family," also was faithful and
enduring. ("Ah, Mammy—valiant and loyal Mammy Callie—
surely never another like you.") But she based her long rela-
tionship with the Falkners on the undefiled assumption that
faithfulness and endurance would be mutual. The Falkners
never violated her trust. When she vanished with "some man
she had run across in one way or another," they waited until
homesick she issued her summons to them. "Weeks would
pass with no word from her when, out of the blue, a train
conductor, traveling salesman, or some local person who
happened to run across Mammy would bring the expected
and welcome word, 'Mammy Callie says this is where she is
and to come and get her.' " Unlike Dilsey, Mammy Callie had

no capacity for detachment and fatalism. She was totally gregarious. Friendly with "everything that stalked the earth," she roamed Bailey's Woods and the town square with an equal feeling of community.

Indeed Mammy Callie personified what in Murry Falkner's retrospective vision impresses us as the dominant aspect of the world of the Falkner boys: community, fellowship, belonging. In the Yoknapatawpha stories we are nearly always aware of strong tensions growing either out of the threats or the facts of irreversible changes in a traditional social structure. Yoknapatawpha is haunted by the mood of estrangement and alienation. Murry Falkner gives us more simply an Oxford filled with the sense of belonging, or, we could say, with the sense of identity. Everybody and everything in this place had an individual meaning. Community was based on a series of interwoven individual relationships maintained in a society that—although it was not an "organization," still less a political-economic-sociological "process"—was more the product of frontier democratic improvisation and compromise than the traditional order we encounter in the Yoknapatawpha world.

In the semi-pastoral world of early twentieth-century Oxford—when American railroading was in its golden age and motoring was in its heroic age—the sense of fellowship encompassed machines as well as animals. Through Murry Falkner's gifted remembrance we see the Falkner boys listening at daybreak to a locomotive struggling up Thacker's Mountain, waiting to hear its downward rush toward the town and "the soul-lilting wail of the whistle" which identified both the engine and the engineer. We see them establishing an intimate rapport with the early automobile, with one automobile at least, their grandfather's fabulous 1909 Buick. The Young Colonel, having seen to it that Oxford had a law forbidding automobiles on the town streets, yielded to the call to adventure and bought a vehicle which had the power to destroy or make a hero out of anybody who challenged it. The section of *The Falkners of Mississippi* detailing the frustrations of traveling in Grandfather's Buick, caring for it, and trying to domesticate it in a horse- and mule-drawn environment is a comic epic. The story of the perilous journey to Memphis deserves a distinguished place in the annals of a day when Americans were united with their automobiles by bonds of an affectionate antagonism similar to that they might take toward a horse or a mule.

Except in his last novel, *The Reivers*, the automobile in Yoknapatawpha is associated with the evils of the twentieth-century wasteland. In *Sartoris* Colonel Sartoris is killed in an automobile driven by his grandson; Temple Drake's lurid saga in *Sanctuary* begins with an automobile accident. So with the airplane, which had its heroic age in the period of the First World War and for some twenty years afterwards. The experimental plane in which young Bayard Sartoris finds death is a symbol of alienation; the flyers in *Pylon* (a novel that bears strongly on the vision of Yoknapatawpha) are "lost and doomed." In Murry Falkner's account of the Falkners and their airplanes, we have a rather different version of the heroic age of flying. He says he and his brothers, all licensed pilots, had a "common and everlasting love" for airplanes. Caught up in the wonder and adventure of flying, they took equal delight in aerial techniques and in the mechanics of fallible, at times cantankerous, flying machines. In trying to define the emotional quality of the attitude Murry Falkner indicates toward the railroad, the automobile, and the airplane, those of us who are old enough may be reminded of the legend of that very resourceful American youth, Tom Swift. Unquestionably his spirit was present, for example,

when the Falkner boys built their unflyable flying machine
out of backyard odds and ends.

Of course the Tom Swift legend is hardly the shaping spirit
of Murry Falkner's remembrance. It seems to me, however,
that there is a legend at the heart of *The Falkners of Mississippi*, a legend at once more ample, more subtle, and more
difficult to define. It suggests itself when we consider the
varied career of the author. A Marine private in France in
the First World War, in the Second an officer in the Counter
Intelligence Corps in Algiers (where he met and married a
beautiful French ballet dancer), a Special Agent of the FBI
for many years, an airplane pilot in the days when flying was
still a highly personal adventure of man and plane—Murry
Falkner has had a career that would have pleased not only
Tom Swift. It is one in which Tom Sawyer would have taken
considerable satisfaction. Realizing this, we are led back, I
believe, to the point I offered about the affinity between the
style, or voices, of Murry Falkner and Mark Twain—to the
essentially literary character of Murry Falkner's quest into
the past. Whatever purposes *The Falkners of Mississippi* may
serve in helping us to document specific distinctions between
the world William Faulkner called his sublimation of "the
actual into the apocryphal" (Yoknapatawpha County) and an
actual Oxford–Lafayette, it is itself a story told by a narrator
of poetic imagination. Murry Falkner does not report sterile
autobiographical and historical facts but an essence of the
past. He evokes the poetry of life, especially family life, in the
world of the American small town (not necessarily altogether
the Southern small town) in the age when this way of life
reached its fullest meaning. This was in the years from the
end of the Civil War to the time of the First World War, an
age when urbanization and technology had advanced far
enough to make the differences between small-town life—

frequently close in the South and West to frontier origins—
and city life something like a cultural absolute. Historically
considered, it was a precarious absolute, but it did exist and
its effects on our culture have been profound, none more so
than the appearance in our literature in all its manifold ways
of the legend that in summation reads: American small-town
youth discovers the great world. Mark Twain developed the
classic form of this legend in his stories about Tom Sawyer
and Huckleberry Finn. Vitally serious as the legend is in our
culture, it is of the utmost significance that it found its great
expression in the voice of Southern and Western small-town
humor. One of the refinements of the legend is the American
small-town youth's discovery of the First World War. In
what has become the classic form of the refined legend, it is
about an American boy who finds the meaning of the war
through the transforming power of a wound, which may be
physical or psychic but is always primarily psychic. His wound
is his badge of membership in the "lost generation" of the
post-war wasteland, a sign, we might say, of the damnation by
which he will live. Ernest Hemingway's hero, called Nick
Adams and other names, is the chief example of this wounded
youth. William Faulkner's young Sartoris is a lesser yet cru-
cial example of the "lost generation" hero. His appearance in
the first novel Faulkner wrote in the Yoknapatawpha saga
foreshadows the prominence, explicit and implicit, of the
"lost generation" and wasteland themes in his fictional world.

On the other hand, one of the voices of William Faulkner is
that of an expansive comic irony that can be traced directly
to the writer he called his literary grandfather, Mark Twain.
It serves in the stories as something equivalent to a redemp-
tion and saves them from pathos of the sort Hemingway's
stories run into occasionally. We think of this when we read
Murry Falkner's account of the head wound he received in

the First World War. After the surgeon removed the last shell fragment from his skull, a nurse gave it to him. "I took it home with me," he recalls, "and handed it to Mother just as it was given to me, on a bloodstained piece of gauze. She kept it, along with my French brigade citation, all the days of her life." Then, a little later on, he recalls: "Several years after the war was over I received at Oxford a small box and a big letter from Marine Headquarters. The one contained a Purple Heart (as everlasting evidence that I forgot to duck) and the other specified where my lack of presence of mind or memory, or both, had caught up with me—Argonne Forest, November 1, 1918." Telling a true story at the level of memory and imagination where historical and autobiographical fact and cultural and personal emotion come together in a fashion defying exact analysis, these two passages in their combination of romance and realism, sentiment and comedy, convention and individualism are more than personal history. The second passage clearly suggests a form of the legend of the stricken American youth in which he is saved from traumatic suffering by the grace of his pragmatic ironic humor. This was a style of life of the world in which he grew up—the autonomous, individualistic world of the American small town, the world of Hannibal, Missouri, and of Oxford, Mississippi. This world is now gone forever. But its dominion in the American mind has by no means disappeared. It was a style of life in which we still seek our identity. This is one reason why we find the world of Yoknapatawpha so compelling. William Faulkner participated deeply in our quest for ourselves. The world of Murry Falkner now becomes a part of our exploration into who we are.

PREFACE

M Y BROTHER BILL PASSED AWAY IN 1962. ABOUT A YEAR
later I happened to see an article in our home-town
newspaper, the Oxford *Eagle*, which set out that Professors
James W. Webb and A. Wigfall Green of the University of
Mississippi were in the process of gathering material for a
book on my brother and were calling upon those who had
known him to submit their reminiscences. Since none could
have known him better than I, at least in his early years, I
felt honor bound (although neither they nor anyone else
ever made an appeal to me) to comply with the request.

This I did by sending them five brief sketches written
on that many different occasions. They became part of the
book which Louisiana State University Press published in
1965 under the title *William Faulkner of Oxford*. The book
was well done, received deservedly complimentary reviews
throughout the country, and is, I think, one of the two best
books on Bill ever written (the other is my brother John's
My Brother Bill, completed shortly before John's death in
1963).

My knowledge of the publishing business is so limited that I was mildly surprised to receive a letter from the editor of the LSU Press explaining that he had sent sections from the forthcoming book on Bill to several New York magazine editors, among them an editor of *American Heritage*, who had expressed a desire to publish one of the sketches I had submitted for the book. Of course I was pleased, but in a sense flabbergasted too, for here I had an offer to sell something I had written to a magazine known to me only by hearsay. And in writing it I had not even followed the good Dr. Johnson's admonition that only a blockhead writes except for money, the sketches having been submitted by me only as a labor of love in memory of my brother.

In the meantime, the LSU Press had asked me to write a book of my own. Having recently retired after more than thirty years of service as a Special Agent of the FBI, I decided to try my hand at it—to write not only about Bill but about my other two brothers and myself as well: the story of a Mississippi family.

To those who have grown accustomed to the name Faulkner, the spelling Falkner may cause some confusion. Perhaps this is as good a place as any to explain how the names of brothers came to be different. The family story, coming down from the previous generation, has it that our great-grandfather, Colonel William C. Falkner, originally spelled the name with the "u," as it had been handed down to him. But after he grew to manhood he dropped that letter, saying that as often as a man had to sign his own name it was folly to keep an extra letter in it that changed neither the look nor the pronunciation. Thereafter he never used the "u," nor did our grandfather, nor our father. And my brothers and I were baptized with water but without the "u."

Later Bill, and in turn Dean and John, changed the spelling to Faulkner. One story is that Bill first used the "u" when he published his first book, a collection of poems. That was in 1924. Another story is that he had occasionally spelled it Faulkner earlier. A conservative estimate would be that I have been asked a thousand times how Bill came to add the "u." My answer has always been, "I don't know." I don't even remember when he began using it, except that it was certainly after he left school. The idea of asking him why he made the change never entered my head, as he was not the sort of man to whom one (at least, not I) would put such a personal question.

John's change to the "u" spelling is much easier to understand. In the early forties he had begun to succeed as a writer, and by that time there were many ready to read after a man named Faulkner.

This brings us, writer and reader, to the present time, when the former hopes there will be at least some ready to read after a man named Falkner.

MCF

Mobile, Alabama
1967

CONTENTS

Foreword by Lewis P. Simpson   vii

Preface   xvii

The Falkners   xxv

1   Oxford—The Early Years   3

2   We Enter School   16

3   "The Falkner Place Is Burning Up!"   31

4   Cowboys, Indians, and a Flying Machine   49

5   The Colonel and His Buick   62

6   "Me and Ed and Jim Will Take On the Falkner Boys"   78

7   There Was a War   87

8   An Inspector Calls   105

9   "I Bare Him on Eagle's Wings . . ."   123

10   A Yellow and Black Aeronca   138

11   A Cow and a Coupe in Alaska   152

12   There Was Another War   171

13   Three Score and Ten, More and Less   186

ILLUSTRATIONS

Following page 74

Falkner family group
Home of Colonel J. W. T. Falkner
Colonel J. W. T. Falkner
Sallie Murry Falkner
Colonel Falkner and his Buick
The Falkner brothers, about 1910
William Faulkner, about 1914
Dean Falkner as a small boy
Note from the Falkner boys' father to his son Dean
William Faulkner and his Waco
Murry Falkner in his Aeronca
Murry Falkner with J. Edgar Hoover
John Faulkner in pilot's uniform, about 1939
Pilot identification card issued to Dean Faulkner
The Falkner boys' Auntee and their cousin Sallie Murry
Murry Falkner's wife Suzanne
Maud Butler Falkner, 1945

THE FALKNERS

William (1897–1962), the author. Changed the spelling to Faulkner.

Murry, called Jack (1899–   ), retired FBI man. Author of this book.

John (1901–1963), also a writer. Followed William's lead in spelling his name Faulkner.

Dean (1907–1935), flyer. Killed in airplane crash.

Their parents

Murry C. Falkner, Sr. (1870–1932)

Maud Butler Falkner (1871–1960)

Others of the family

J. W. T. Falkner, Sr., called Colonel (1848–1922). Grandfather of William, Murry, John, and Dean.

Sallie Murry Falkner (1850–1906). The boys' Granny.

Holland Falkner Wilkins, called Auntee. Daughter of Granny and the Colonel. Mother of Sallie Murry Wilkins (the boys' cousin).

William C. Falkner, called the Old Colonel (1826–1889). The great-grandfather. Author of *The White Rose of Memphis.*

And Mammy Callie Barr (1840–1940).

THE
FALKNERS
OF MISSISSIPPI

OXFORD—THE EARLY YEARS

WHEN WE MOVED FROM RIPLEY TO OXFORD, MISSISSIPPI, in the fall of 1902, my brother Bill was five, I was three, and John was barely one. The two towns were only about fifty miles apart in a straight line, but that wasn't the way folks traveled in those calm and unhurried days. Our father brought the household goods by road in wagons, and Mother brought us by train, over the railroad built by our great-grandfather Falkner, from Ripley (where John and I were born) to New Albany (where Bill had been born in 1897), then over the Frisco line to Holly Springs, and the Illinois Central on to Oxford.

The better part of two days was needed to make the trip by train, and I remember how oppressively hot it was and how we were pelted incessantly by cinders from the stacks of the little passenger locomotives. The windows of the wooden coaches were kept open to provide fresh air which, though filled with swirling cinder flakes, was better than none at all. What a trial it must have been for Mother, an eternal enemy of dirt and disarray in any form. But Bill and I were in a sort of little boys' Seventh Heaven, for even then the never-to-end love for trains was upon us and it mattered not that we were covered with soot, cinders, and sweat, our hearts were overflowing with happiness and excitement.

We arrived at Oxford after dark and were met at the station by our grandfather and grandmother Falkner with some of their servants to aid in getting us to Grandfather's house, where we were to stay until Father arrived with the family furniture. We descended from the coach, and Bill and I were speechless with wonder; never had we seen so many people, so many horses and carriages, and so much movement everywhere. And the lights—arc lights! The first we had ever seen. As we drove to Grandfather's house by way of the town square we noticed the fine board sidewalks which extended the whole way. More than that, people were walking along them and it was already past nine o'clock at night. We could hardly wait to see these wonderful sights by daylight.

Though it could hardly be regarded as a population explosion when we moved to Oxford, we did add five to the thousand or so folks already there. Mother was, in a sense, coming back home: she had been born and reared in Oxford. Our grandfather and our Uncle John had come there to live a few years earlier. Both of them, as well as our father, had attended the University of Mississippi, which was then and is now situated on a beautiful tract of land about a mile west of the town square.

Before moving to Oxford, all of the family had resided at Ripley or New Albany, within sight and sound of the rail-

road which Colonel William C. Falkner had built after the
end of the War Between the States. He was our great-grandfather, whose title came from the rank he held in the army
of the Confederate States of America. He had been a lieutenant in the United States Army in the war with Mexico
and was elected colonel of the 2nd Mississippi Infantry when
it was organized in the spring of 1861 to fight for the Con-
federacy. For his actions on the field at First Manassas he received a personal citation from General Joseph E. Johnston,
the Confederate army commander. The regiment continued
to serve with the Army of Virginia and when the next elec-
tion of officers was held, the following year, the Old Colonel—
who was not much of a hand at wet-nursing his soldiers, or
anyone else for that matter—was voted out of office. He returned to Mississippi and organized a troop of cavalry.

The Old Colonel was a man of diverse accomplishments.
He had been a soldier, he was a lawyer, and he was the author of several books, the best known of them *The White
Rose of Memphis*, which was to come back into print more
than a half century later when two of his great-grandsons attained recognition as writers. One, Bill, used to say that he
wrote to support his small and unself-supporting farm near
Oxford, which was in keeping with the tradition of the Old
Colonel's writing to support the building of his railroad from
Pontotoc, Mississippi, to Middleton, Tennessee. The building of it was a remarkable feat when one considers the circumstances which existed at the time. No southerner came
out of the war with any money, and the Negro was now free
and under no compulsion to dig a roadbed and lay ties for
anyone, especially since no one then had the money with
which to pay him. Even so, black and white lent a hand,
and the railroad not only got built but stocked and set in
operation.

The Old Colonel had a partner in the venture. In adversity they worked shoulder to shoulder; in the prosperity that came with the completion of their project, they became enemies. Duels were an accepted, indeed an inescapable, way of life in those days, and the Old Colonel had been victorious in those in which he had engaged. The end came for him without challenge or warning as he was conversing with a friend in front of his former partner's office on the little town square in Ripley. Standing in the door to his office, the man aimed and fired one shot, which hit the Old Colonel in the mouth and took his life. That was in 1889—eight years before his great-grandson Bill was born.

While Bill built no railroads and took part in no duels, I always felt that he more or less unconsciously patterned his life after the Old Colonel's. He spoke of him often, and it has been said that, as a child, he was asked what he wanted to become in life and he replied, "A writer, like my great-grandfather." This answer attributed to him was certainly in accord with his character and his dreams.

Of course, there had to be a Young Colonel. He was our grandfather, John Wesley Thompson Falkner, and the title was given him in memory of his father. There was never any confusion when we were growing up. We never had to ask, "Which Colonel?" There was only one: our grandfather.

The Colonel was a lawyer before he took up banking. And he looked like we thought a lawyer and banker ought to look. In the summer he wore a big panama hat and a black alpaca coat. His was a commanding figure, set off by a heavy gold watch chain running from pocket to pocket across his vest and a stout, gold-headed walking stick. He was hard of hearing in later life, and, when sufficiently prodded by Granny, would carry an old-fashioned horn hearing aid. When he was approached by some talkative and insistent citizen whom he was temporarily unable to fend off, he would insert the small end of the hearing aid in an ear, growl, and say "Hah," then aim the flared-out end at the would-be conversationalist. How much he actually heard he alone knew, but I always had the feeling that he managed to hear what he wanted to hear and totally disregarded the rest. I'm sure that had I dared to say as much to him, he would have first glared at me, then smiled, said "Hah," and patted me on the head. He loved his family and his country, the latter meaning, of course, the South. He had been born in 1848 and therefore had a clear recollection of the good life of his kind in our state before the War. He saw his father take his regiment to Virginia, lived through the years of shining victories followed by defeat, and saw his beloved country devastated even more by the carpetbaggers in peace than it had been by the enemy soldiers in war.

His speech, odd at times even to our ears, was that of any educated man of his generation. For instance, he always pronounced the word "are" as if it were spelled "air." How often have I heard him recite bits of children's poetry to us, as we sat on his big front porch after nightfall. I can hear him now saying, "Twinkle, twinkle little star, how I wonder where you air." I never heard him complain about the War, but he spoke of it frequently, always referring to his father as "Kunnel Falkner."

Grandfather and Grandmother Falkner lived in "The Big Place" on South Street, and with them lived their only daughter, Holland, whose husband, Dr. James Porter Wilkins, died two years after our arrival in Oxford. Two years later Granny died, and our aunt stayed on to look after her father. She had one child, our cousin Sallie Murry. Throughout our childhood Sallie Murry and Bill and John and I could not have been any closer had we been sister and brothers. We played together in our homes and ranged South Street from one end to the other, flying kites, shooting marbles, skating, and playing our homemade brand of hockey.

Sallie Murry's mother we called "Auntee." Dear Auntee:

what Falkner privileged to know her could ever forget her. Surely no more fiercely loyal member of the clan ever lived. She it was who became an unmistakable character in a number of Bill's stories: the one whose steadfast devotion never wavered, whose everlasting love never lessened, and whose pride of family was so intense that she sustained and supported the other members no matter what misfortunes they brought upon themselves as a result of their uncontrolled impulses, lack of judgment, or just plain orneriness.

Auntee was a remarkable woman and was in every sense what the storybooks call "a lady of the Old South." She knew one "cuss" word and used it with gleeful abandon when circumstances were such that none other would suffice. That word was "damn" and it was invariably used by her to connect with and precede the word "Yankee," though her pronunciation of it, plus the fact that it always meant the same thing, left me under the impression for years that the two words were in fact only one.

We were of a common conviction that had Auntee lived at the time of the War, the South would never (could never) have lost it, seeing that the Yankee had us outnumbered by only three or four to one. Surely Auntee would have made up this trifling difference without half trying. Ten or twelve to one would have put some strain on her, but anything less would have been unworthy of serious thought to one of her temperament and loyalty. She knew nothing of the War firsthand, but she did live through the years that followed—the so-called Reconstruction period. I don't know what the carpetbaggers from the North reconstructed, but it wasn't Auntee.

After we moved to Oxford, Grandmother Butler (Mother's mother) lived with us until her death in 1907, shortly before our little brother Dean was born. She had much artistic talent and was always busy at her easel when not helping Mother run the house or watch over my brothers and me. Mother told us that shortly after the War some northern art society, noting her mother's talent, had offered to send her to Italy to study, but that Damuddy (as we called her) had declined.

Damuddy was a Baptist and her religion was an intense, personal part of her life. She was unfailing in her kindness and affection for us all, though it seemed plain to me that I was the recipient of most of her attention. This I felt resulted from her compassion: she must have believed that of the three (then) of us, the going was to be the toughest for me. Evil was beyond her ken, the Bible was her constant companion, and I'm sure that Heaven was her final home. She suffered much to reach it. Her death was due to cancer and in those days even less was known about it and how to treat it than is known today. I never heard her complain and never saw her cry, even during those last terrible months when her ever-increasing agony could have been supported only by a faith that never faltered.

Mother and her brother Sherwood had been left without a father to support them when they were still children. Jobs for women then were few and far between, and Mother became a stenographer when few women entered the world of business in any capacity. She went on to graduate from the women's state college at Columbus.

Mother was small in stature (special orders had to be made for shoes small enough to fit her), but she was ten feet tall in will power and determination. Certain it is that she had a great deal to do with what sort of men her sons became. Nothing, to her, was smaller and meaner than for an individual to complain about his own shortcomings and apparent misfortunes. Characteristic of this conviction was a cardboard placard hanging above the stove in her kitchen as long as I can remember, on which she had written in red paint in her neat, clear brush strokes, "Don't Complain—

Don't Explain." It was, in a real sense, her philosophy of life, and she passed it on in full measure to her children.

She had an abiding love for literature and that, too, she passed on to all her children. She was really touched by much of what she read. I have many times seen her on the verge of tears over one passage, while another would cause her to chuckle in unabashed delight. She never tired of reading the ancient writers—Plato, Aristotle, and the like, but she was just as quick to take up the more current ones. We had a Malay edition of Joseph Conrad that became dog-eared through almost constant turning of the pages. Other favorites of hers were Rudyard Kipling and James Branch Cabell.

Our father loved railroads and found happy employment on the one his grandfather had built before we moved from Ripley. He loved horses, too, and found equally contented employment in running a livery stable after we came to Oxford. It was an easy life and a pleasant one for him, I'm certain. He had his office at the head of the livery stable, a gang of Negroes to attend to the horses, two white men to drive the hacks, and always two to ten cronies to sit about the comfortable stove in his office and tell tall tales about animals, hunting, and fishing, applying themselves to the ever-present crock of good drinking whiskey as the mood and thirst struck them individually and collectively.

One of his men, Mr. Jones—in top hat, long-tailed black coat and long, string bow tie—had been driving a hack to meet the incoming passenger trains for longer than anyone could remember. I'm sure that Father would no more have thought of running the livery stable without him than he would without the horses. Mr. Jones came of an old family, once wealthy and affluent. At about the time his family descended to near poverty, another local family, as though on the opposite end of a seesaw, went from pure poverty to considerable affluence. The father of that family died and the son engaged the hack to drive him to the cemetery. The son had not forgotten the early days and wanted to be certain that Mr. Jones noted the present. En route to the cemetery he called to Mr. Jones, riding high on the box that served as the driver's seat, "I see that you are driving me to my father's funeral." Without turning his head or batting an eye, Mr. Jones replied, "That's fitting—he drove me to my wedding."

With the coming of automobiles the livery stable business began an immediate and steady decline. Father finally gave it up, and his father, as was customary, aided him in acquiring another business, this one a hardware store. It was never particularly successful, one reason being that Father was not a natural-born salesman—of hardware or anything else. In fact, he told us several times that he never heard of a Falkner who could sell a stove to an Eskimo or a camel to an Arab. Neither did I. However, even though the business failed signally to make us rich, it presented no insurmountable problem to Father's continuation of his pleasant way of life. The store was less than a block from the old livery stable, the office was bigger, the stove warmer, and there were more chairs to accommodate his ever-present cronies.

Eventually, to the surprise of no one, least of all to Father, he had to give up the store. Shortly thereafter he was appointed secretary and business manager at the University of Mississippi. We moved into a pleasant old brick home on the campus and Father entered on his duties at the University. The twelve years he spent there were, I'm sure, the most agreeable of his life.

As I look back over the years, I realize how little I actually came to know him, and, perhaps, even less to understand him. He was not an easy man to know. We called him "Dad," and he addressed us by our Christian names or, in my case, by the name "Jack," which he gave me as a child for reasons I never knew, if indeed there were any. He would use the intimate "y" or "ie" ending when speaking to us sometimes, but not almost invariably as Mother and Damuddy did. As might be expected, he was the unquestioned head of his own household, and on occasion laid his hand heavy and firm upon it, but never upon us. None of us ever received physical punishment from him or from Mother, but it was always the gentle hand of the latter which guided us along the road of Christian conduct. Whether our father felt that this was the natural province of the mother or whether it was because she was always at home and he was not, I do not know.

He never discussed his personal or business affairs with others—at least, not in our presence. In his youth and early manhood, before the family sold the railroad, he was at once its station master, treasurer, and vice-president. His scale of accomplishments did not reach such heights in Oxford, but he could certainly always reflect that few men become vice-president of a railroad at twenty-five.

On the other hand, his good qualities were legion and they, too, did much to mold the characters of his sons. His word was totally dependable. For instance, if he said that he would be at a certain place at a certain time, nothing short of sickness or death itself could have prevented his being at the exact place and at the exact time he had designated. His capacity for affection was limited, but I'm sure that to such extent as it allowed he loved us all.

There was one other member of our household—Mammy Callie Barr, who came to us shortly after we arrived in Oxford and continued as an honored member of the family until her death nearly forty years later. Mammy had a formidable imagination, a good memory of the "old days," and kept Bill, John, and me (and later Dean) spellbound with her stories. Surely from her came many of Bill's writings about events in Lafayette County, especially those dealing with whites and blacks.

The "Mammys" of that time were women who, with everlasting devotion and loyalty, became second mothers to white children and in so doing became intimate and loved members of the households where they were employed. Of them surely none gave more of her affection and varied talents and was loved more in return than Mammy Callie. Like our mother she was small in size, and, also like our mother, big in will power and a sense of right and wrong. It was understood that, while Mother always had the last say, we were never to disobey Mammy Callie. And we never did—at least, not for long.

Mammy was not considered a servant by the family or by herself. Her small, old-fashioned rocking chair was for her alone and always beside the fireplace. There she would sit in the evenings, as much a member of the family as any of the rest of us, high-button shoes (how small they were) polished and glistening in the dancing glow of the flames in the open grate, her box of snuff in place on the mantel just above her head, a good layer of it tucked beneath her lower lip and her "snuff stick" held firmly in her mouth.

She had been born in slavery, could neither read nor write, and did not know her age, but from what she told us about life in Mississippi before and during the War she must have been at least in her teens when it started. (The stone which Bill placed over her grave gives 1840 as the year of her birth.) She had her cabin in our backyard, and Mother kept it supplied with what she needed and wanted. When we were little we would often visit with her to listen while she told us of the old days. I think Mammy felt a kinship with every living thing, that is, those she saw day in and day out and could reckon with: humans and small animals such as dogs, cats, squirrels, and rabbits. These she knew and they were the subjects of many delightful stories that poured from her bright and active imagination.

Her friendly familiarity with everything that stalked the earth was particularly noticeable in her personal protocol of addressing those she considered worthy of it by their Christian names or titles, or even by both at the same time. There was an attorney in town whose first name was William, and Mammy always addressed him as "Mis't Lawyer Will." Grandfather was "de Kunnel" when she spoke of him, and simply "Kunnel" when she spoke to him. Grandmother Falkner was "Mis Sallie," and the proprietor of the local dry-goods store was "Mis't Ed." If the word "gregarious" had not already existed, someone would have had to come up with the likes of it for Mammy. I have seen her on a street corner, neat, friendly, and completely at ease, talking to some business or professional leaders of the town, and when I returned along the same street a short time later I would see her one block farther along, in cheerful and animated conversation with some cooks and maids from nearby homes. England has had its King Edwards, and I'm sure that had Mammy had the occasion to become acquainted with one, and he the good fortune to know her, she would have affably and completely unself-consciously addressed him as "Mis't Kaing Ed" and he could not have taken affront.

She had several grown children living in the western section of the county, her original home, and they would visit her from time to time. If none came for a while, Mammy would tell Mother and some of us would take her out to call on them. She knew every human being who resided within walking distance of her home—white and black, young and old, rich and poor—and she called on one exactly like the

other whenever the notion struck her. I'm sure that all profited by her visits, though it may well be open to question, in
some instances at least, whether she would not have been better off had she stayed at home. I remember how, when we
were children, she would suddenly take off with some man
she had run across in one way or another. One such trip took
her to Tennessee, one to Arkansas, and another to the Mississippi Delta. The outcome was always the same: pretty soon
she was longing for home. Unable to write, she had to get a
message to Mother or Father by word of mouth. Weeks would
pass with no word from her when, out of the blue, a train
conductor, traveling salesman, or some local person who happened to run across Mammy would bring the expected and
welcome word, "Mammy Callie says this is where she is and
to come and get her."

Had the matter been left entirely to Father, I'm sure he
would have let Mammy stay put for a while. But the rest of
us missed her too much and Father was outnumbered. It
would end up, of course, in his sending an emissary to fetch
Mammy home. This worked everywhere except once in Arkansas. Father's friend came back and said that he had gone to
the small town named by Mammy and searched the surrounding plantations high and low, but found no trace of her. So
Father had to go to look for her himself. It isn't likely that
his livery stable business suffered greatly from his absence;
still, he could certainly have found other things more agreeable than going to some unknown town in Arkansas to look
for Mammy after his friend had already failed to find her.
Actually it wasn't very far away, just across the river from
Memphis and, unexpectedly enough, the only living thing
he saw at the station on descending from the train was
Mammy, happy and friendly and wanting to know, "Mis't
Murry—when does us git home?"

2 WE ENTER SCHOOL

HOW KIND THEY WERE, THOSE YEARS OF LONG AGO; HOW gentle the life and how pleasant the memories of it. I can almost see us now: the day is done and we are all about the fireplace in the living room—Mammy in her rocking chair, Father with the paper, Mother sewing, and Bill, John, and I listening to Mammy telling us again and again about the War—still, as always, the only one. We were all there, each belonged, was loved, and loved in return. Mammy called us collectively "mah white folks," an affectionate and honored title as was the one we used in addressing her. To her, Father was "Mis't Murry," Mother was "Mis Maud," Bill was "Memmie," John was "Johncy," and I was "Jackie." When he came along, Dean was "Deanie."

On other evenings (motion pictures had not yet come to Oxford, and radio and television were many, many years away) we read. It was Mother who gave us our love for literature—literature in any form that would entertain, broaden the mind, and make us aware of past history and present events. She had already given us a good working knowledge of English before we entered school, and our room was filled with children's books of the period. Any question that stumped us Mother was ready to answer, straightforward and clear.

When we soon outgrew children's books, we turned to more comprehensive reading matter. There was always a daily newspaper in the house (the Memphis *Commercial Appeal*), *St. Nicholas Magazine*, the *Saturday Evening Post*, the *Youth's Companion*, the old *Life Magazine*, *Collier's* and the *Delineator*. There was no public library in Oxford then—books were supposed to be in the home. In ours I remember James Fenimore Cooper's tales of the American Indians, Dickens' works, *Treasure Island*, Pepys' *Diary*, *Amos Judd* (Mother's copy was the only one I ever saw or heard of, and the author, then editor of the old *Life Magazine*, never wrote another book; but the one he did write was, to us, a small masterpiece), *Robinson Crusoe*, Grimm's fairy tales, *Uncle Remus*, Mark Twain's books, *The Virginian*, and a number of books about the War. Later, as we advanced in school—and at the always-encouraging hands of Mother—we began a lasting acquaintance with the works of Kipling, Poe, Conrad, Shakespeare, Balzac, Hugo, Voltaire, Fielding, and many others, each of whom brought enlightenment and pleasure to three boys in a small Mississippi town more than a half century ago.

What we read in our youth is set out in some detail because the question has often been asked, "What did William Faulkner read before he began writing?" He read all of the books and periodicals named, as well as others doubtless long since forgotten by me, and probably others unknown to me at the time. It has been said that literate friends guided his selection of what he read. He had such friends, and I'm certain he would not have disdained any suggestions they might have made, but he was perfectly capable of making his own selections, and I'm certain that, to a large extent, is what he did.

I remember that Bill and John and I could read and thoroughly understand the sports page before any of us entered school, which meant that, in a very real sense, we cut our literary teeth on baseball box scores. Bill entered the local grammar school in 1905, Sallie Murry and I the following year, and John in 1908. The grammar and high schools were in a single brick building, and the principals changed but rarely, the teachers never; that is to say, everyone who taught one of us taught us all, each in turn. There were no busses to take us to school or anywhere else. Besides, no child lived beyond easy walking distance of the school, and this included going back home for the midday dinner.

Bill and John and I would leave home together en route to school, each carrying his satchel containing his books, ruled tablet, and big yellow pencils. In the early fall and late spring we were usually barefooted, as were all the other small boys. At such times we walked in the dusty or muddy street so as not to run the risk of picking up a splinter from the board sidewalks. Occasionally Sallie Murry joined us when we passed her house, but not often. Being a girl, she always wore shoes and thus found the going easier, and certainly cleaner, on the sidewalks no matter the weather.

There may well have been another reason why the girls stayed strictly apart from the boys. The school was two blocks beyond the northwest corner of the town square, and this was the recognized area where the boys attended to any unfinished personal business from a previous day, such as a full-fledged, bare-knuckle scrap which had left neither antagonist completely satisfied. There they would meet again, and each knew that they would "have at it again" on sight. A small ditch separated the sidewalk from the road, and as soon as the two boys spotted each other they would carefully lay their satchels on the plank sidewalk, then step off and face each other on the shoulder of the ditch. This left the road open to traffic and the walk to other students having no business more urgent that day than going to school. As soon as the boys squared off, the girls knew as well as anyone else what was going to happen, but decorum required that they continue daintily on their way and not even appear to be interested in what was about to take place. The other boys, of course, were not under any such restrictions, and they quickly gathered in a happy and expectant ring around the two then mightily engaged in flailing away earnestly at one another. Sooner or later both would be down in the ditch and the one on top universally acclaimed the winner. Then all on to school for another day.

My recollection is that, at least during the early years of our schooling, the classrooms were heated by wood-burning iron stoves. And since the students were seated alphabetically, I did an inordinate amount of fretting during the cold winter months about why my parents had not had the foresight to chop the "F" off our name and thus place me among the "A's" and nearer the stove. Even so, such inconveniences were trifling. The teachers saw to it that we profited from our attendance at school, and Mother saw to it that we profited even more at home.

Though Bill and John had to do much less studying than I did (sometimes, in exasperation and envy, I concluded that they really had to do none at all), Mother saw to it that we applied ourselves to the morrow's lessons every evening after supper. She would place a freshly cleaned and refilled oil lamp on the center of a round table in our bedroom, which meant that the study hour had arrived. The three of us would seat ourselves about the table, and each would neatly stack his textbooks at his left elbow and carefully open the top one at the appropriate page. Then, depending on how far Mother was out of earshot, we would undertake to widen our knowledge or fall into a spirited discussion of our ponies, a recent baseball game, or some other equally important subject.

There was another ritual always performed by Bill: the placing of his open-blade pocket knife in the center of the table, for he knew from long experience that I was probably the champion pencil sharpener of the whole county, maybe the whole state. I had found at an early date that a distraction, however temporary, furnished a remarkable relief to a clogged brain; and sharpening pencils was one of the best of all, being one of the few things that one can do without thinking at all. Mother had already caught up with me and put a permanent stop to my going to the kitchen for a drink of water every ten minutes or so.

Finally, the long study hour would come to an end, even for me, and thereafter we were free to do as we pleased until bedtime.

There was no such thing as central heating during the early years of our residence in Oxford. Each room in the house, except the kitchen, had a fireplace. In cold weather (and there was such from time to time during the winter months) fires would be made in the grates of the bedrooms. How pleasant it was on such nights to lie in bed, after the lamp had been extinguished, with the quilts pulled up snugly beneath the chin, listening to the cold rain against the windowpanes, the warm and caressing glow of the fireplace reaching up and out as it enveloped the whole room from floor to ceiling.

When we arose on a winter's morning the cheerful fire of

yesterday had become cold and cheerless ash. Bill, John, and I would grab our clothes and scurry into the living room, where a lively fire awaited us. We would waste little time in dressing and even less at the washbasin, unless Mother or Damuddy was present to make sure that we at least splashed some water on our faces. Having somehow gotten through this most unwelcome but unavoidable chore, we would charge into the dining room for breakfast, which was always an important meal for the whole family. There would be coffee for the grownups and hot chocolate for us, both topped with whipped cream almost as thick as butter. Then there would be eggs and country sausage, or ham or bacon, and, best of all, hot biscuits or pancakes or waffles. Toast was practically unheard of, for the simple reason that all loaf bread was baked at home and it was considered too unusual for anyone to even think of burning the sides of it. There was a wide variety of jams and preserves, all homemade, during the summer and fall.

Once in a while there would be the rare treat of oatmeal, and that too had to be prepared at home and without haste; no one in those days had ever heard of such a thing as the three-minute variety. Mother, not the cook, always prepared it at night by putting the meal into a double boiler, which was set over a banked fire in the stove to simmer until the next morning. A serving would be placed in a bowl, sugar added, the bowl half filled with fresh cream with the consistency of molasses, then topped off with as much thick whipped cream as the eater figured he could manage, and we managed an awful lot of it with no trouble at all.

There was also ever-present on the table that delight to any true southern gullet—sorghum or cane molasses—without which we would not have considered the table as being set. It was all homemade in the county, and the Negroes called it "long sweetening" to distinguish it from common sugar, which they called "short sweetening." Many farmers had small areas set aside on their farms to grow the cane, which was harvested and taken to a central mill for extracting the juice. The mill was central in the sense that it was on a farm in the neighborhood where those living nearby could take their cane to be processed. There was a metal vat surrounded by a circular wall of bricks. Attached to an upright shaft in the center were the rotary blades. A long wooden pole extended out horizontally from the top of the shaft and at the end was a clasp to which were coupled the traces of a harness. A mule furnished the motive power for operating the rotary blades, pulling the long pole as it made a fixed circular path around and around the vat. This operation always took place in late fall, by which time the weather had become cold enough to cause the breath from the mule's nostrils to vaporize into small white plumes as he trudged patiently around and around in the fixed circle.

This was also "hog killing time." Nature's cold was needed to protect and keep the hog meat, since no such things as freezers or refrigerators existed. There was another means of preserving food on farms where there was a natural spring on the place whose constantly running water was quite cold the year round. A small bed, inlaid with brick, would be built just in front of the bubbling spring outflow. Rows of brick would be set along each side and a small dam erected at the far end to control the height of the water. This would allow the constantly flowing cold water to reach just to the necks of the glass jars containing milk, cream, eggs, and butter and would keep them cool and fresh for an almost indefinite period.

We lived in town and had no spring; therefore, in common with our neighbors, we had to depend on the "ice box" to keep such food fresh as required refrigeration during the long,

hot summers. It was aptly named: There was a compartment
at the top for the ice and underneath it was a larger one for
the food. Depending on the size of the compartment, the box
could hold from about twenty-five to one hundred pounds of
ice. Each home with an ice box also had a small, square card
on which was printed 15, 25, 50, and 100 lbs. Attached to the
center of it was an arrow which could be set to show the
amount of ice desired that particular day. The arrow would
be appropriately pointed and the card hung face outward on
the front porch. The "ice wagon" passed each morning; the
driver would note the amount needed, chip a cake to that size
in the wagon, and then put it in the ice box on the unlocked
back porch.

Sunday was not only the Lord's Day, it was ice cream day as
well. When we had all returned home from church Mother
would prepare the ingredients for freezing. Sometimes there
would be fruit, but for the most part it would be just plain
delicious vanilla or chocolate. In any case, the cream used
would be as thick as molasses on a cold winter day. While
Mother was making her preparations Bill, John, and I would
crack the ice and get out the sack of granulated salt kept for
this happy event. Then the mixture would be poured into
the freshly scrubbed cylinder of the freezer, ice would be
packed around it and covered with salt. The three of us would
take turns at the freezer crank handle. As the mixture chilled
and became increasingly stiff, more and more force was
needed to turn the handle, but none of us ever complained.
We had only to reflect on the marvelous treat that would soon
be before us and, a little later, inside us.

During these early years Bill and John and I went regularly
to Sunday school at the Methodist church. Though none of
us ever became confirmed churchgoers in later life, we all considered the existence of a Supreme Being as unquestioned;

and each tried, in his own way and according to his own conscience, to follow the precepts of the Ten Commandments.
Once Bill said to me, a few years before his death, that perhaps
each of us will become a sort of radio wave in the hereafter. I
think what he meant was that he found it as difficult as I to
arrive at a reasonable concept of another life at all similar to
that we have known here on earth. That another life could
be physically the same as this one seems impossible, or at least
totally beyond human comprehension. Not only that, but the
conception of time in the hereafter must be reckoned (if indeed it is reckoned at all) on a basis entirely different from
anything we know or can imagine.

There can be no question, as far as I can comprehend, but
that the vast, incredible reach of the universe bears the hand-
marks of a Maker. The exact orbits of the planets, the life-
giving warmth of our sun, the alternate periods of light and
darkness and of heat and cold, living things upon our planet
and the availability of nourishment to sustain life, our own
bodies with their incredibly intricate organs of sight, hearing,
assimilation of food, manufacture of life-giving blood and its
circulation, muscles to move us about, mind to enable us to
think, the ability to reproduce our own kind—all of these
things are too precise, too orderly and purposeful to have just
happened. Yet, there remains the simple, unanswerable question of the child, "Who made God?" We have only to look
about us to see that all of these things exist, and it seems to
me that they could exist only as a result of an intellect so vast
and so all-inclusive that none of us who result from it can do
more than contemplate, be amazed, and attempt no more to
understand it than He who made them intended for us to
understand. Perhaps this is what is meant when the Bible
admonishes us to have faith. We can do no more, and it would
be folly to do less.

Religion was a real factor in our lives when we were growing up. Mother had been a Baptist, but we were baptized in the Methodist church. Camp meetings were held regularly throughout the county during the summer months. They were religious in nature, and whole families would spend several days at them, attending services and visiting with friends and acquaintances present. The camp meetings were occasions for monstrous consumption of food, the ladies vying with each other in the production of delicacies. So plentiful was the food laid on the community tables and so frequent the opportunity to partake of it that one could not help but wonder how the good ladies found time to devote themselves to the services, though it could certainly be said that those who did were embarking upon salvation on full stomachs.

Another place we would visit during the summer months was a big two-room cabin which Father, Uncle John, and some of their friends had built on a lake northeast of town. It was called "The Club House," and we went there frequently to spend several days at a time—grandparents, parents, children, and some of the family servants. There were no automobiles in Oxford yet, and the trip was made in buggy and surrey, with the supplies brought by wagon. It seemed at the time and under the conditions to be a trip of considerable distance. I was soundly surprised a few years ago to find that the site of "The Club House" is less than nine miles from the town square. No matter—getting to the place in those days was an expedition, and staying there was an adventure wonderful beyond the telling. The lake teemed with fish and the surrounding countryside with animal life—rabbits, squirrels, foxes, and even some bear and deer. There were also snakes, which was the reason that the cabin was built on poles about ten or twelve feet above the ground.

Bill, John, and I had Daisy air rifles which were quite powerful, but we were allowed to use them for nothing more than shooting at stationary targets or occasionally at a snake sunning on a log near the edge of the lake. The grownups had some of the newfangled fishing rods that worked with the line running through them which was controlled by a reel. Bill hit upon the idea of manufacturing one for his personal use. Under his direction we selected and cut a long bamboo reed while the grownups were fishing from the boats on the lake. We took the reed out behind the cabin, and Bill explained that he was going to make a hole running the length of the reed so he could put a line through it. He planned to do it in one fell swoop by shooting a pellet from his air gun through the center of the cane, from one end to the other. I still don't know why holding the cane did not fall to my lot (as such jobs usually did), but somehow John ended up holding the long cane at one end while Bill, at the other, pressed the barrel of his rifle close against the head of the cane and pulled the trigger. The small pellet could not even dent the core of the cane, which Bill was probably holding at a slight angle anyway; it glanced off the cane and headed for the next thing in line, which happened to be John. It swiped a smart groove across his knuckles, and he let out an "Ouch!" Mother and Father were in a boat not far off shore and, hearing John's high-pitched yell, came in a hurry. Mother later said that our father could not have made better time had he suddenly developed the ability to run on water.

We loved the woods and Mammy loved to take us there, which was not hard to do in the early part of the century in Oxford: one needed only to step out of the back door. We went "bird-nesting" in the spring, and Mammy taught us to recognize the birds on sight. We would spot a nest, then shinny up the tree to get eggs for our collection. Most of that work fell to Bill, who was the strongest and most agile. Those halfway up a tree I would get, while those on the lower branches were left for John. In the fall we would return to the woods and gather hickory nuts and walnuts which we would take to Mammy's cabin in our backyard. Mother would furnish us with some big peppermint sticks, Mammy would build a big fire, and we would eat and talk the rest of the day. Here, as I recall it, Bill began telling tales on his own, and they were good ones, too. Some of them even stopped Mammy, and she was a past master in the field if ever there was one.

Calmness and serenity spread a benevolent benediction on Oxford during the years of our growing up; haste was easily avoided, leisure was an accepted fact of life, and no man stood on any feet but his own. Such commerce as existed was given attention only after it was no longer needed for personal matters. None there was brash enough to consider that the customer was always right. On the contrary, unless he was both prudent and patient, he was universally judged as being wrong, especially if he dared to interrupt the flow of conversation between the proprietor of the store and his cronies seated about in various comfortable accommodations. The tales they told were on the tall side and were judged not for accuracy but solely on effectiveness of delivery. A man was not even admonished if he told the same tale twice, provided it sounded as good the second time as it did the first.

All of this applied only to the men. When a woman entered a business establishment on the town square it was to buy something for which she had desperate or at least pressing and immediate need, resulting from her inability to talk some of her menfolk into getting it for her. While the good lady had little hope of getting any more cooperation from her husband downtown than she was able to wrangle when she had him under foot at home (which was almost never), she was practically certain to stumble upon him if her shopping quest brought her to enough of the stores, since as a matter of custom and inclination he was bound to be sitting contentedly with his cronies in one or another. He may even have had to inconvenience himself to the extent of easing his chair over a few inches so that his wife might get by in order to make her purchase. This could not be reckoned to lead to any appreciable marital bliss at the moment, and could be calculated to lead to still less come evening, but it did indicate that the wife had found, as most had to find sooner or later, the one sure way to get something done for the house.

One who lived during that period is brought to wonder why the world was so much quieter then than now. Maybe it was because there were fewer noisemaking machines, or men might have been just simply less garrulous. I remember that especially during the early afternoons (when few moved about) and at night (when none did) one could easily hear the lonely and plaintive call of the bobolink deep in Bailey's Woods. The bell in the town clock at the courthouse literally reverberated throughout the community as it tolled the passing hours. One's attention was seldom distracted from his own home, and therefore one had little occasion and less desire to concern himself with what transpired a thousand, or even a hundred, miles away.

In those quiet days before the affliction of radio and television, Oxford also managed to get along well enough without bridge clubs (or any other sort for that matter) or corner taverns, and there were few shows and fewer public meetings. Entertainment, aside from that of the close-knit family circle, was for the most part along the established lines of folks just simply visiting each other. A family would have its calling cards, and on a small table just inside the front door would be a neat silver tray to receive them. All went strictly according to what I'm sure Emily Post would heartily pre-scribe. Having called and been received and seated in the parlor, one did the only thing there was to do—talk. The ensuing conversations were elegant, in the sense that they were on a higher plane than offhand, back-fence gossip and considerably more dignified than the dialogue usually preva-lent on the town square. Besides, one could always look for-ward to the ritual of tea or coffee and delightful homemade cakes.

When a friend or acquaintance called, deportment required that he be received with courtesy, offered food or drink, and made to feel welcome. His obligation went a little further—he was supposed to know when to depart. I remember the tale of one visitor who might reasonably be said to have run an undue risk of overstaying his welcome. As the story went, and I heard it a dozen times, the visitor was a bachelor who lived alone in Oxford and was the last of his line. He decided to visit a friend who lived about ten miles out in the country. He set out on horseback early one morning and arrived at his friend's home that afternoon. The family received him with wholehearted welcome, brought him drink as befitted an honored guest, and bade him be seated in the parlor. He accepted both—and remained for eleven years, or until the last member of the family had died and there was no one left to be his host.

The story certainly had much factual background, assured by the temper of the times, place, and people. We knew the visitor well, and, after he had moved back to town, Bill and I were standing on the south side of the square one day and fell to talking about the monument to the Confederate soldier located on a pedestal just south of the courthouse in the center of the square. Original plans were to set it on the north side of the courthouse, but Granny, always active in affairs in com-

memoration of the War, was outraged and would have none
of it, insisting that a southern soldier, even in granite, should
be on the south side of anything (in this case a matter of some
two hundred feet or so) and should face the south. It might or
might not have been beside the point that her home was two
blocks south on South Street. Anyway, as in most things, she
prevailed, and the statue was erected on the south side of the
square facing in that direction, where she could see it from
her home on any clear day. As Bill and I were discussing the
statue, we noticed the long-term visitor standing alone and
quiet before it, slowly reading the inscription which he had
known by heart for twenty years or more. I asked Bill if he
thought the man had actually remained as a guest at the home
of his friends for eleven years. Bill glanced at the monument,
the man before it, and the people moving unhurriedly about
the placid square. Then he chuckled and replied that he hoped
so, that any less time would be an injustice to the man and
the story.

3 "THE FALKNER PLACE IS BURNING UP!"

IN 1905 WE MOVED TO A HOUSE ON SOUTH STREET, A FEW doors down and across the street from our grandfather Falkner's house. Our new home had a big yard and a long, deep pasture extending back past the barn. Between the house and the barn was a small one-room building which we turned into a playhouse.

Painters had been busy about the place, and after their departure our father, in a singularly thoughtless moment, remarked that several cans of red paint had been left over. It turned out to be a day without profit all around, for even Mammy Callie went placidly about her work indoors without frequently checking on what "dem boys" were up to, as

was her wont from long experience in dealing with us. We got
the cans of paint from the tool shed, took three old brushes
from the barn, and brought them to the playhouse to begin
the inevitable. Sallie Murry happened by about that time.
Usually she took a wholehearted part in almost everything
we did, but one glance told her what we were setting out to
accomplish and, being a girl, she wanted no part of it. On the
other hand, events promised to be interesting, so she sat down
on a nearby sawhorse, eating a piece of cake she had acquired,
and cheerfully prepared to watch.

Bill was, as usual, in charge of the project, and under his
supervision John and I dragged up two ladders which we
placed against the side of the playhouse, the larger one on the
outside and the smaller one below and on the inside. Then
Bill climbed to the top of the big ladder. I was beneath him
on the smaller one, and John, who could not reach the side
of the house from even the small ladder, stood on the ground
beneath me. The three of us were now in a vertical row,
each with a can of bright red paint and a dilapidated brush.

We set to work with hearty good will (after all, it was our
playhouse and no one had thought to say we couldn't paint it)
and soon what had to happen began to happen. Before it was
over I doubt if Sallie Murry ever enjoyed an afternoon more
—or if Mother and Mammy enjoyed one less. Bill was the only
one wearing a cap and, under the circumstances, turned out
to be the only one having no need for a head covering, for
within a few moments the paint from his brush began dripping down on me, and that from both our brushes continued
down onto John. Until we took up house painting John and
I had brown hair (his almost blond), but now it quickly became bright red, as did our eyelashes and eyebrows. John was
the littlest and, no doubt, suffered much in his determination

to follow his older brothers. Rarely did he complain. Now he did and with reason. "I'm tired," he said, and promptly sat down on the ground beside the ladder. The weight of a gallon of house paint escapes me, but it must be considerable. Whatever it amounts to, approximately two gallons could have been added to John's natural weight. He was completely covered with paint; only his clear blue eyes were visible, and his shirt and trousers were so thoroughly streaked with paint that it was difficult to determine where one ended and the other began. About this time one of Mammy's friends happened by, saw us, and shouted to her, "Callie Barr . . . Callie Barr! Git yo foot in yo han', come a'runnin' an git dem chullen out'en de backyard. Fo de Lawd, ain't no injun ever got hisself redder!"

We could hear Mammy hurrying through the kitchen to the door leading into the backyard. "Lawd a'mercy, Ah maht a'knowed things wuz too quiet!" As she pushed open the kitchen door she saw us and hesitated only momentarily to throw her hands above her head in consternation and outrage. It was a goodly number of paces from the kitchen door to the playhouse, and Mammy had now picked up speed again after the few seconds' halt at the door. More would come from her later, much more, but as she hurried toward the playhouse, her kerchief quivering on her head and her clean, crisp apron switching about her high-button shoes, her ire was too high and what she saw too unbelievable at the moment for her to do more than repeat, "Lawd a'mercy, Lawd a'mercy." We were fascinated by the cadence—left foot, "Lawd," right foot, "a'mercy," right until she stood before us, all five feet and one hundred pounds of boiling rage. Now she began to really talk and she talked right at us: "You Memmie an Jackie—git down Ah's tellin' you all—git down from dem ladders an drap de paint. Whut in de Lawd's name is you tryin' to do—drown yo little brudder in hit? Ah asks you—look at Johncy on de groun an him up to his neck in de paint. Who gwine know him now—who gwine say he ain't already daid? Eff'in Ah tells yo daddy (we knew she wouldn't and she knew she wouldn't) he gwine sho'ly git a scatlin an whups you all 'till you wishes you wuz daid too."

Then gingerly she walked over to John, holding her apron above the paint-splattered ground, and gently held out her hand to him. "Git up, Johncy," she said quietly, "Git up an come wid me." Then to Bill and me in a tone altogether different, "An you all too. We'se gwine ter see yo mammy rat now, but don't git close 'nuff ter slosh de paint on me."

By this time the commotion had reached Mother's ears and she too came to the kitchen door and looked with dismay at our handiwork, but even the sight she beheld never interfered with the orderly process of her mind. Mammy, muttering to us and to herself, was towing us to the kitchen door—John, myself, and Bill, who were, in order, covered with the glistening red paint, splashed and covered, and simply splashed. As we arrived at the bottom of the steps leading up to the kitchen Mother said for us to stand still, not to move a foot, and for Mammy to come into the house and help her. We were allowed to enter the house only after Mother and Mammy got some old newspapers and spread them all the way from the kitchen door, through the lower floor, up the stairs and on into the bathroom on the second floor.

Mother had already decided that Bill, always the leader, was the most reprehensible. Mammy was sent forthwith for a two-gallon can of coal oil and on her return Mother's plans began taking shape. John was undressed and put in the tub first; then, under Mother's watchful and strict supervision, Bill and I had to swab him down with the coal oil until such of the paint as could be washed away was washed away; this was followed by a bath in water as hot as he could stand. My turn for the same treatment followed, then Bill's. Finally, as a little extra punishment, Bill had to wash the red paint out of the tub after we were through. It was a distasteful project at best, and I think the memory of it lingered with him for years. As we grew to manhood it developed that he had much artistic talent. I recall seeing some of his fine paintings before he gave it up completely. I have wondered, in idle moments, if what happened when we set out to paint the playhouse did not inculcate in him a sort of disagreeable distaste for the brush which lasted his lifetime.

I recall another incident in which our childhood energies produced a great amount of far-reaching excitement. Our father, knowing our love for steam locomotives and being unable to provide us with one, did the next best thing: he gave us a small, stationary steam engine. It was light, easy to move about, and would work. The single piston operated a drive shaft which turned an axle with a small pulley wheel at each end. Steam was generated from the water in the boiler by a little kerosene lamp attached to the bottom. There was a safety "pop-off" valve and even a shrill whistle. We set up the machine on the floor of the playhouse and used it to run all sorts of contraptions that we rigged up to operate off the small pulleys. It took a lot of figuring, which was supplied by Bill, and a lot of work, which was supplied by Sallie Murry and John and me.

One day we were busy running a new gadget that Bill had developed when something, I know not what now, diverted our attention and activities to the north side of the yard. We had been there a few moments when Sallie Murry happened to glance back at the playhouse. What she saw made her call out, "Look—the engine has set the playhouse on fire!" One look told us that it had indeed. We sprinted back to it and found that the flooring planks were enveloped in flames. Mammy, whose apprehending senses never missed anything for long, burst out the kitchen door and sped toward the playhouse with her apron flying in the wind as she called over her shoulder to Mother, "Mis Maud—Mis Maud, git de fiah folks (fire department), dem chullen is burning us out of house an home!" Then to us, "Lawd a'mercy, Ah ain't nevah see sech chullen in all mah bawn days. Take a eye off'en you one minute an you burns up de whole place. Git a bucket—git some water—git a broom!" Bill and I bolted to the kitchen door to meet Mother coming out with two small buckets filled with water. We doused it on the flames and put them out, but not before a good citizen who happened to be passing in the street had seen the commotion and, unknown to us, had quickly closed the three short blocks to the town square and passed the word of a fire to the "fiah folks."

Mammy was right: there was a fire department, numbering about ten or twelve more or less active, civic-minded citizens of the community, supposed to be always on tap in case of a fire. The fire wagon, an appalling greenish pink in color, would actually hold some water which could be useful in fighting a fire, provided it did not all leak out before the wagon could be got to the scene of the flames. Motive power for the wagon was two mules, stubborn and contrary in keeping with their kind. The designated fire chief was sitting—not thinking, just sitting—in front of his store on the square when he got the word, "The Falkner place is burning up!" This brought him to some attention, but totally missed eliciting any commendable clarity of thought, since neither he nor any other member of that good group thought to ask which Falkner, and in those days the section south of the town square was filled with them.

The first members of the crew to reach the firehouse began

filling the fire wagon with water, while the others, aided by little boys who suddenly appeared with gleeful anticipation from all over, started out to round up the mules. Now, strictly speaking, anyone who has ever lived in the same county with mules can verify that you do not exactly round them up: it is more like begging, cajoling, cursing, pulling, pushing, and ultimately calling upon fate for help; and, even then, it is not the man who gets the mule to go anywhere, it is the mule which just decides to go some place. By this time perhaps a half-hour had passed and, of course, the fire had long since been extinguished, which unhappily was unknown to both fire fighters and mules. After making seemingly determined false starts north, east, and west (known to be false by the mules all the time), they finally elected to go south, hauling the fast-emptying fire wagon and the valiant fire fighters at a reasonably steady and purposeful clip. The dusty street got a good sprinkling from the now almost depleted water tank and all arrived at Grandfather's house; after all he was a Falkner, but he wasn't afire and did not know one who was.

The worthy crew came upon the Colonel down at his barn. They were all fellow citizens, had come abroad to do favor to him or some of his clan, were manifestly in want of something invigorating to drink, and he kept a good stock in the barn. They welcomed his thoughtless invitation and promptly fell to depleting his liquor supply with warm and appreciative gusto. All were thus happy and contented until some extraordinarily conscientious soul happened to remember what they came for in the first place. This reactivated the original mission, put the earnest band on the highway again, and actually got them to Uncle John's house. He too was at home, and he too had a little drinking whiskey.

In going from Colonel's house to Uncle John's they had passed right in front of our place. Indeed, several hours later one mule and the pink fire wagon were still in the street directly in front of our gate. The other mule had shed his harness and disengaged himself from the whole affair and the wagon. The one left with the fire wagon and then dragging it around and around in a tight circle in the middle of the street could, of course, have taken off as well and as easily as the other. The difference was that for the time being he was stuck with the determination to do exactly what he was doing.

By this time the fire in the playhouse had been extinguished for two hours or more; still, such excitement doesn't come every day and our backyard was filled with folks from all over town. Indeed, the only ones missing were those valiant "fiah folks" who were supposed to have come to put out the fire in the first place. In brief, Uncle John had some firemen who had no fire, while we had a fire which had no firemen.

But not even the fire could match the excitement of that day a man was to go aloft in a real balloon. Oxford had been on edge with this exciting news for weeks, and surely none were more keyed up with anticipation and wonder than Bill and John and myself. We were determined not to miss this momentous event. We knew that our father would either be at work or watching the balloon himself, that Mammy Callie would be helping Mother about the house, and that Mother had paid no more attention to stories about a balloon than she would have to rumors about a visitor from Mars; so all we had to do was to ease out the back door and hurry up South Street the short distance to the square.

On reaching it we beheld a sight never to be forgotten: an enormous grayish-black bag was attached by ropes to stakes set in a circle on the ground, in the center of which a hole had been dug for the fire which was to produce the smoke to inflate the balloon. The fire was already burning briskly, and, though an almost overwhelming amount of smoke was blowing into the eyes of the onlookers, it seemed that at least some of it must be causing the gentle billows within the bag itself. All of this was being administered by the crew—an incredibly dirty and surly white man and a very tall gangling Negro, whose job, so far as we could see, was to furnish fuel for the fire and drinking whiskey for the white man.

By noon all the horses and mules had been removed from the square, partially to save them from blindness and partially to provide more room for the ever-increasing number of townspeople who were happy to risk it in order to see what was going on. By this time the fire was a roaring one, but still the balloon was not more than half inflated. The spectators were covered with soot and John, happy though he was, had some misgivings. "Just wait 'til Mother sees us," he said. Bill reassured him, "Don't worry, she won't recognize us." Now the greasy smoke was pouring out from under the bag and we could barely make out the white man sitting on a keg beside the raging fire. When the wind blew the smoke away for a moment, we could see him take another swig from the crock and dash another bucket of coal oil on the crackling flames. We wondered how he could live in such a place. Bill said that the man had probably spent so much time enveloped in smoke that good fresh air would likely kill him.

Although a tremendous amount of heavy smoke was swirling about the square, some of it was manifestly rising within the balloon, which had begun to sway back and forth and tug at the restraining ropes. We could see some smoke spewing out of several breaks in the fabric and, because the Negro was so tall, we could see him towering above the smoke clouds as he went languidly about closing the ruptures with clothespins. By this time Bill and John and I were covered with black,

greasy soot, tears were streaming down our faces, and we had
never been so excited and happy. We had to be careful though,
for Mother had sent Mammy Callie to get us. We could easily
hear her as she pushed through the crowd calling out, "Where
at dem Falkner boys?" Then louder, using her name for Bill,
"Memmie-Memmie. Yo' Mammy says where at is us all and
git home." We stayed put and did not reply; nothing could
have dragged us away.

By now the motley crew had attached four ropes to the
basket which was to hang beneath the balloon and carry the
pilot, or whatever it was that individual called himself. It
took considerable thrashing about to get the white man and
his crock aboard. During the process the basket was dragged
too close to the flames and one rope was promptly burnt
through, leaving the basket canted over on one side with the
pilot lying on his back and taking a good swig from the crock
the while. Thick black smoke was pouring from the fire, and
the balloon was straining at the ropes. We were beside ourselves with excitement. The pilot took the crock away from
his mouth long enough to yell at the Negro, "Cut, damn it,
cut." In a second the Negro became a flying dervish. With axe
in hand he charged the restraining ropes one after the other—
swish pam, swish pam, swish pam. His transformation was
amazing. We could see his head and shoulders above the
billows of dense black smoke as he slashed a rope, then darted
to the next one, slashed it, and so on until the last one had
been severed. Smoke seethed; we were rigid with attention
and anticipation. The balloon slowly began to rise and we
could easily hear the pilot cursing the canting basket, the
smoke-spewing balloon, and, very likely, the general laws of
physics as well. Anyway, he was airborne, and, as soon as the
craft rose above the buildings on the square, a gentle north
breeze set its course a little east of due south, toward our
home. Bill sensed it at once, caught John by the arm, and

called out, "It's going directly over home—let's go." Lots of other folks had the same notion, but they rushed headlong down South Street. We took a short cut, every foot of which was known to us.

We squirmed through the crowd and scurried down the wooden steps and into the lot below Brown's store. Now we were on our own—alone and streaking across the lots and gullies between the square and our back lot. We realized quickly that it was tough to run headlong over the rough countryside and look up in the sky at the same time. It took us weeks to get over our collective skinned knees, hands, and faces, but we had to follow the flight of the wonderful balloon, not having any idea as to its cruising range, altitude, or speed. One astounding thing we learned pretty quickly was that the thing had very little forward speed. Indeed we were out-running it. And, more than that, it was already beginning to lose altitude. In fact, it was moving so slow and so low that we were suddenly shocked to realize that the pilot, still stretched out full-length on the low-hanging side of the basket, was talking right at us between swigs at the crock. We could not make out what he was saying, but he was certainly addressing us, as we were the only ones in sight. Now we had arrived at Mrs. Powell's fenced-in backyard, where that good lady had chased us out of her apple trees often enough. This time she was waiting for us on her back steps, but she hadn't yet seen the balloon, and we didn't propose to lose it, fence or no fence. Bill never hesitated, knowing that where he went we would follow. We shinnied over the fence and pulled John along with us, then charged across the yard to the fence on the other side. The lady must have seen us a split second before the balloon came into view. She gathered her apron about her, waved her duster at us, and called out, "William Falkner—you boys stop right—" then, "Oh my Lord," as she suddenly noticed the low-flying, slow-drifting balloon, with the cursing pilot on his back in the canted basket, drifting silently across her yard. It was truly fantastic. As we scrambled over the fence on the far side of her yard, Bill said that if we could have had a balloon overhead every time we had been in Mrs. Powell's orchard she never would have caught us taking green apples.

By this time the marvelous craft was barely floating over the treetops, and our back lot was just beyond. As we climbed up and out of the last gully, we saw that there were two people near our barn, Mother and Mammy Callie. The latter, not having to contend with the balloon every step of the way, had beat us home and was doubtless explaining to Mother that she couldn't find "dem boys" on the town square. Mother was not often in the back lot, but was there this time seeing about some flower stands that one of the handymen had built for her and left near the barn for the paint to dry. Our three ponies were standing in a row behind Mother and Mammy, being the most docile of beasts and given to following any member of the family like the pets they were.

Now we had climbed over the last fence and were in our own back lot, and we could see that the balloon was certainly going to land there. We hesitated but a second in reflecting that, if we continued on, we would find ourselves face to face with Mother and Mammy. But it couldn't be helped: we had lived with this splendid aircraft too long to give it up before the end—which was fast approaching. There was a quick and heavy swish just above the chicken house, and the ponies instantly looked skyward. They backed off, stamped their feet, and shook their heads in disbelief. Mother followed their gaze and saw it too, just as the collapsed bag enveloped the barn and the basket plunked down on the roof of the chicken house. It dumped the pilot out onto the roof on the back of his neck; his hand made a big arc, smashing into the shingles and breaking the crock he was holding, and whiskey poured down on the unsuspecting chickens calmly at roost below.

Instantly they set up a cackling that could be heard a mile away. The pilot slid gently off the roof and onto a pile of hay beside the chicken house. Mother and Mammy were transfixed, but not for long. Mother said, "This man may be hurt." But Mammy was all action in a very respectable endeavor—she was setting out to protect her folks. She grabbed a scantling, longer than she was tall, and muttered. "Eff'in he ain't hurt, Ah garntee he gwine ter be." She charged toward the pilot stretched out on the hay and drew back the scantling. As she did so she saw Bill and John and me standing beside the chicken house, clothes torn, covered with soot, and scratched all over.

For once in their lives Mother was shocked into speechlessness and Mammy into frozen immobility. Mammy's feet were set far apart, she was stretched to her full five feet in height with the scantling held by both hands high above her head, and she literally seethed with anger and astonishment. This was a sight to sober even the pilot who, seeing his chance, quickly rolled away from the chicken house, jumped to his feet, and bolted with a speed and precision that put his wonderful balloon to shame. Mother recovered her speech and, seeing that Mammy was set to haul off in hot pursuit of the pilot, touched her on the arm and said, "Mammy, let him go." Then they turned and looked at the three ragged, dirty little Falkner boys. Mammy dropped the scantling, turned to Mother, and said, "Mis Maud, what we gwine to do wid dem boys?" We knew the answer to that one, yes indeed we knew.

It was about this time that the first automobile came to town. It was coming from Jackson, a hundred and seventy miles away, and within less than ten days it had arrived at Water Valley, only eighteen miles distant. Two days later the progress report said that it would arrive at Oxford before the day was done, maybe even before nightfall. Whatever time it came it would have to pass up South Street, right in front of our house, and we were determined to see it—as was everyone else in town. People had talked about it for weeks. Front porches and plank sidewalks were crowded from noon on with men and boys and a scattering of womenfolk and the air was filled with excitement, but voices were subdued lest we fail to hear the motor of the car as it came up South Street hill.

Darkness had fallen when we first heard the "chug-chug" of the motor and silence and intense concentration settled over the multitude, or rather the approximately one thousand souls who lived in Oxford then. The sound of the exhaust became stronger as the car labored up the hill just south of town; then we could tell as it reached the crest and gathered speed, doing perhaps all of fifteen or twenty miles an hour. Now its headlights came into view, the first any of us had ever seen except on a locomotive. In a few minutes the car was passing beneath the arc light in front of our house. It had been a dry season, thick dust billowed from beneath the tremendous rubber-tired wheels, and we were all enveloped in a choking, swirling cloud of it. Even so, as the machine passed beneath the arc light we could make out the enormous bulk of it. The top was down, and there were two men on the front seat and one lone passenger in the rear. All wore the stiff straw hats of the day, dust-saturated raincoats, and goggles. The gentleman in the rear was smoking a large cigar and, though it was not until later that we realized it, the glowing end of the cigar actually made more light than the carbide-gas lights flickering feebly in the big headlights.

Before the coming of the automobile, folks traveled by train if they traveled at all, and those living in our neck of the woods almost invariably had the same destination—Memphis, Tennessee. It was big, it beckoned, and, comparatively speaking, it was not far away. The first daily north-bound passenger train came through Oxford about four o'clock in the morning.

We would arrive at Holly Springs, some thirty miles distant, in about an hour and a half. There we would eat breakfast at the lunchroom in the station while we waited for the Memphis-bound Frisco train due in at six o'clock. The Frisco crossed the Illinois Central tracks (by which we had come from Oxford) just north of the Holly Springs depot, coming in from Alabama to the northeast. I remember how, with our father, Bill and John and I would walk up and down the station platform as day was breaking, listening carefully for the first sound of the approaching train, each hoping to hear it first. Then, as though carried over the rolling hills by the soft and gentle rays of the rising sun, the sound of the wonderful whistle on the locomotive would be upon us—faint, far, and unforgettable. At first sound we would instantly stop in our tracks. None spoke. All listened. What was it about the whistle of a steam locomotive that so utterly fascinated and captivated our father and us? Whatever it was, the effect was the same on each of us. Then we were aboard the train bound for Memphis.

In those distant days, there was a busy establishment located about fifteen miles from Memphis known as the "Keely Cure," which would not only make a man shun good drinking whiskey but would actually keep him away from the bottle, sometimes for several weeks or even months. Our father, in common with a goodly portion of the rest of the male members of our clan, was singularly free from any aversion to the bottle, and this led him, from time to time, to become a guest at the Cure. Mother had to get him there, and on several occasions Bill, John, and I were taken along too, because we had to stay somewhere during her absence from home and there were facilities available at the Cure, even though it was not exactly a family spa.

A streetcar line served the Cure from Memphis. Pending

and during treatment the guests could not avail themselves
of it. But the attending families, being more or less on their
own, were bound by no such restrictions, and excursions on
the cars furnished Bill and John and me with some memorable experiences, especially when we were allowed to go
on them alone. All we had to do was to promise Mother that
we would stay in the car and not leave it under any circum-
stance until it completed the round trip. As a matter of fact,
there was little possibility of anything untoward happening
to us; we were perfectly content to sit, look, listen, and ride.
There were never many other passengers when the small
four-wheeled, open-vestibule car clanged out for Memphis;
thus, in a sense, we could not have been shrouded by more
apparent affluence had we been riding in a private railroad car.

It was a genuine rural ride for the first thirty minutes or
so, the car clicking, clacking, and gyrating through woodlands
and across fields and meadows. But all this changed as we approached the city. We began to cross fine, well-dragged high-
ways where we could see lines of vehicles, mostly horse-drawn,
but with a commandingly prestigious automobile here and
there. The steadily thumping generator of the car would
make the wide-eyed passengers pulsate in their springless,
rigid wooden seats, and the wheels would clatter over the light
and uneven rails, while the motorman stamped with authority
upon the floor pedal which actuated the sharp-pitched, clang-
ing warning bell. My guess now (sitting at a desk three hundred and seventy-five miles away and fifty-some-odd years
later), is that the small thumping car was probably doing all
of eight or nine miles an hour, but at that time, in the excitement and imagination of youth, it seemed to be rushing upon
the city at an incredible speed.

Soon we were in the immense and wonderful city itself,

skimming along a track running up the center of a broad avenue. Sometimes we could count as many as four or five vehicles moving spiritedly along on each side of the streetcar. Large, imposing residences lined each side of the street, and passengers entered or left the car in every block. These were real city folk, and we were prepared, if called on, to welcome one and all—provided none got between us and the window through which we were observing all the fine, moving sights. John it was who, one never-to-be-forgotten day, happened to glance across the aisle and happily announce a sight that held us spellbound. It was a fleeting glimpse of the Mississippi River. We all stood up to get a better view and what we saw almost stunned us with excitement. A number of boats and barges were tied up at a wharf. It was the first time we had ever seen a boat, or water deep enough to support one.

The Cure must have done a considerable business. Back in the good old days, at least in our part of the country, liquor was an accepted way of life as far as many of the menfolk were concerned. Few women would touch it on pain of certain and universal condemnation by the community. This did not mean that men were taught to indulge in it, any more than they were instructed to rise when a lady entered a room, to lie only when it would be of great value to another, or to take pride in their family and their country. These things—the drinking, the code of personal conduct and philosophy of life—were simply passed on from generation to generation by manners and deportment, no succeeding one having sought or found a more agreeable way to live with his fellows.

Mother detested whiskey, and it was forever beyond her understanding how a man could bring himself to partake voluntarily of something which contrived only to make him a bigger fool than nature had done in the first place. Unfortunately, this did not deter our father any more than it did most of the rest of us in later life. The tale persisted in Oxford even after we moved there of how Father, when a student at the University, would give vent to his exuberance after taking a few drams by charging around and around the campus on his horse, just as Bill was to do in an airplane in Canada some twenty-five years later.

4 COWBOYS, INDIANS, AND A FLYING MACHINE

MOVING PICTURES! PICTURES THAT MOVED! HOW START-
ling was the news of such an incredible accomplish-
ment in the early years of this century. The first ones that
came to Oxford were shown at the Opera House—admission
five cents. Some of them, I remember, were one-reel western
starring "Broncho Billy."

The show would begin (when the projection machine
worked) promptly at seven o'clock in the evening. The dim
lights in the theater would be extinguished one by one (the
manager having to go to each and yank on a dangling cord),
then a cone of white light would shoot out from the projector
and across the tops of the heads of the audience. A sign re-

quested the ladies to remove their hats, but even so the beam would pick up the uncovered heads of the taller customers and project them in an uneven line along the bottom edge of the screen. At that point the operator would begin to crank the film through the projector and a big black daub would splash against the screen, as though someone had thrown a bottle of ink on its vertical surface. This was the signal for the man at the piano to crash into the opening bars of what I suppose he took to be a tune calculated to put the audience into the proper mood to appreciate the hoofbeats of horses soon to appear before their very eyes. The opening scene in the westerns never varied. (So many of the westerns did we see that eventually we came to realize that all scenes were taken at the same place and under virtually identical circumstances.) There would be, in the distance, an enormous cloud of dust. The dimensions of the cloud may have changed from picture to picture, but the background—never. It was a sizeable mountain range and we came to know it so well that we could have drawn a contour diagram of it to minute scale with our eyes closed. The dust cloud held to its size and volume and soon we could make out the first of the fleeing Indians, lying flat on the backs of their ponies, whose flying hoofs were keeping perfect time with the piano player, or perhaps the other way around. My brothers and I used to wonder what would have happened to us and the rest of the enchanted audience if the movie folks had gotten mixed up one time and let the cowboys blast out of the dust cloud first with the Indians chasing them. Probably we would have run out of the Opera House.

Later on, during the pleasant evenings of the summer months, movies were shown at what we called the "Air Drome." It was set in a small depression just off the southeast corner of the square. Starting time remained the same, but customers came early. After all, what better place to sit and discuss events of the day than a pleasant, central meeting place where the cool breezes were free and seats cost but five cents. As twilight began to envelop the community the citizens would begin moving leisurely toward the town square and the show—singly, by couples, or in whole family groups.

On such evenings when we were allowed to see the movies at the Air Drome, Bill, John, and I usually left home right after supper and set out, each with the nickel price of admission in his pocket. Small boys went barefoot in the summertime, and by preference we walked the few short blocks down the middle of the dusty road. Seldom, at that hour, was there any traffic in the street to bother us. A farmer in his mule-drawn wagon getting a late start home or a spirited pair of high-stepping horses pulling an elegant family carriage might be seen on occasion; otherwise we had the road to ourselves as we trod happily along up the dusty street, Bill and I on the outsides and John in the middle.

Seating arrangements at the Air Drome were quite comfortable for some, less so for others. Some regular seats had been brought from the Opera House and set up near the screen and in the center of the plank floor. Elsewhere, there were wooden benches on the floor and in tiers along each side and at the back. Actually, so far as we were concerned, there was no pressing reason for us to arrive beforetimes, for no matter when we arrived, we were going to end up sitting on the planks. Those were the days when children were not only taught to always defer to their elders, especially the women, but invariably practiced it; so no matter how many real seats remained unoccupied when we arrived, we bought our tickets and then popped up on one of the top tiers of planks with

other boys of our age group. There we would talk, eat pop-
corn, and try to contain ourselves until the movie flashed on
the wide, if rickety and uneven, screen.

Youngsters of today take the movies for granted, if, indeed, they take them at all. But for us, more than a half
century ago, they provided a vast new field of incredibly attractive entertainment. This was especially true in such a
small town as Oxford. Moreover, the very newness of them
had an appeal that comes seldom in a lifetime. Their educa-
tional or cultural value was zero, but those of us who went to
see them, and that included practically everyone who could
walk and possessed a nickel, had but one idea—to be enter-
tained. Though we were frequently disillusioned, we were
rarely disappointed.

Aside from moving pictures the only away-from-home
amusements were the circuses that came to town, usually in
the early fall, and the "live" vaudeville shows that came to
the Opera House several times each year. As for the marvelous
circuses, almost all citizens of the community could talk of
nothing else after the coming of one had been announced by
the great colored posters put up on walls and fences all over
town.

The circuses always traveled by train, and the train was
set on a sidetrack at the station. How thrilling it was to see
the cars being unloaded. The circus roustabouts handled the
unloading, and we concluded that they were a tough lot.
Heretofore when someone wanted us to do something different from what we happened to be doing at the moment, the
request would be made in a gentle tone and usually followed
by the motivating word "please." Not the roustabouts,
though. Here, for the first time, we were not asked to do
something in a courteous and agreeable manner, but were
ordered by style and words that almost froze us in our tracks.

The man said, "Hey, you damn kids over there—git—scatter—git the hell out of the way!" He certainly shocked us, but it was a two-way street. Where he could be amiss in politeness, we could be just as short in accommodation; so we stayed put, narrowly escaping decapitation by swinging tent poles and being crushed by large horses and larger elephants. They were indeed grand and exciting days, and when they were over we were as tired as the performers.

The vaudeville shows were actually minstrel shows. All the performers except the master of ceremonies wore burnt cork makeup to make them resemble Negroes. The routine changed but little from show to show and, I suspect, the jokes not at all. The principal members of the cast sat in a semicircle on the stage, and each in turn did his bit of singing or dancing under the prodding of the interlocutor. There was a man! We tried awfully hard to follow his rapid-fire delivery, failing frequently; and we tried even harder to pronounce his title, failing always. It isn't likely that the manager of the show would have permitted the curtain to rise until his actual head count assured a profit, but this problem never came up at Oxford. My recollection is that every seat was occupied by an expectant audience long before curtain time.

What else, in those far-off years, did a boy growing up in Oxford do for entertainment? Once we built an airplane. Nothing else that we did during those years do I remember quite as vividly. We had never seen a plane, had no models or blueprints to guide us, yet we contrived to build what must have been the first one in the state of Mississippi. Pictures of them we had seen and pored over, as they had begun to appear at infrequent intervals in the newspapers and magazines of that period. As far as design and manufacture were concerned, the problem of a motor stumped even Bill's vivid

and productive mind, but his ample inventive scope easily encompassed a small openwork, wooden cage (designed to carry a pilot) which was attached to a wing to get and keep him airborne. The minor detail of how to get him launched into the air would be worked out as the craft was being constructed.

Having decided upon the manufacture of an airplane, Bill had only to select the materials and draw up a design for it. Sallie Murry, John, and I constituted an always-on-tap labor pool, just as when, under Bill's close supervision, we redesigned the interior of the tool shed to resemble a locomotive cab and rearranged the area under the big elm tree in the side yard to conform to his version of the lumber industry in Canada. He called us into the carriage shed on a pleasant summer day and carefully explained the project. We took this to be an endeavor worthy of our talents and, listening to Bill, the scheme appeared to incorporate no insurmountable barriers. Still, we were a trifle apprehensive, for our collective memories were not barren of instances when some of his projects had brought us much diligent and sustained effort— like the time the fall before when we had worked like beavers to dam Bailey's Creek. Bill had assured us that diamonds awaited discovery in the bed of the creek, needing only four or five days of backbreaking work to get to them. Needless to say, we found none.

We were not exactly skeptical either, for we had seen a locomotive run and a tree cut down, but this plane project involved the manufacture of something of which we knew only second or third (maybe only fourth or fifth) hand. In short, we were prepared to give strict attention to Bill's explanation, but it had better be both good and convincing. Had we been a little older at the time (we ranged from eight

to twelve years) I suppose we could have saved our breath and
Bill's time, for he could explain anything, anywhere, anytime. As it was, he told us about the aircraft we were going to
construct. It was just like a kite, he said: wind got it off the
ground and wind would keep it up. He gave short shrift to
the question of a motor (which was just as well, seeing we
could do nothing about one anyway), saying it was not worthy
of serious consideration, at least not until after we had made
some trial flights, after which we might install a pedaling
device like a bicycle if we decided to fly higher and longer.

He went on to tell us that he had figured out that a square
yard of paper would get and keep a four-ounce kite airborne;
therefore all we had to do was to build the wings and the
"cage part" (we had never heard of an airframe or a fuselage,
either) which we would carefully weigh to arrive at the exact
number of square yards of paper needed to support the whole
works. As was usually the case, his explanation was so convincing that we could detect no flaw in it, but a grave and
shocking one, at least as far as I was personally concerned,
cropped up in his concluding remarks as he casually announced that I would be the first pilot.

I was eager and willing to work, but totally lacked any
inclination to find myself a target for the application of the
old saw about some men having fame forced upon them.
True enough, I was certainly not very well known, not beyond the confines of South Street anyway, but I would need
a little time to reflect on this fame-courting business, especially since I had not been consulted about the job. So I promptly
protested the honor. For one thing, I had no experience (there
probably were not a dozen men in the whole country who
did); for another, the airplane wasn't my idea in the first
place; and finally, I said, I had just as soon share the glory

with someone else or, better still, anyone who wanted it could have it all. Bill waited me out patiently, as he usually did, then out-argued me completely. There would be great glory in it, he assured me, and a fine opportunity for me to exhibit my pioneering spirit.

With Bill as straw-boss we set out to construct the flying machine in the carriage shed, though none of us had the slightest acquaintance with, much less any idea as to the meaning of, words such as "wing lift," "center of gravity" (or even plain "gravity"), or "dihedral." However, there was no lack of building materials; strips of wood, some less rotten than others, were all over the lot in all shapes and sizes; rusty nails, big and small, were had for the pulling of them from planks, and Sallie's and our homes yielded enough old newspapers to cover a dozen wings. But a complication arose right off the bat. We found that the newspapers would not hold together long enough to be nailed onto the wing frames, which put us to looking for some heavier material. We came up with a number of discarded grocery sacks and some old wrapping paper, but not enough of either to cover the two wings in Bill's biplane design.

Then back to our drafting board on the sawhorses in the corner of the shed, where we evolved a new set of figures—a subtraction here, an addition there, and a multiplication where one seemed appropriate or unavoidable. All of this, plus the fact that there were no more sacks and no more wrapping paper, forced us to discard the original biplane theory and give serious thought to a single-wing affair. When Bill announced that such would indeed be the case, I promptly protested again, this time that I had been apprehensive enough about the chances of two wings keeping me airborne and now was faced with the necessity of risking my neck with only one. Bill had a ready reply, but somehow it seemed to lack conviction; after all, it was my neck that was to be laid on the chopping block of progress and invention. He said that a single wing would be big enough to support the weight involved after we had knocked a few planks off the "cage part" which was not absolutely essential anyway, and that I could do away with even more weight by leaving my cap and shoes on the ground before takeoff. If we could find a higher ditch to use in shoving the craft off into flight, it would quickly get on top of some good, solid air and the ensuing flight would be mere child's play. I was a child all right, perhaps no more than a mere one, but the project was beginning to look less like play all the time. I would personally have chucked the whole thing without further ado, but there was no place to which I could run and hide, seeing that we were already in our own back lot.

Under Bill's steady and apt supervision, including a frequent check of our scrawlings on the drafting board, and with the diligent application of Sallie Murry, John, and me to hammer, saw, and baling wire, our magnificent flying machine began to take shape. Mammy Callie, with our little brother Dean in her arms, would visit us to pass the time of day and to see what was going on. She would carefully sit down on one of the empty boxes that were kept for guests, generously replenish her lower lip with snuff, cross one brightly polished, high-button shoe over the other, begin to rock Dean gently in her arms, and commence talking. She naturally wanted to know what we were constructing, and we just as naturally told her. This must have been the first time she ever heard the word "airplane," and we took some pains not to explain what we planned to do with it, knowing that in such case she would likely put a stop to the project at once. Also, we knew that the idea of a flying machine had never entered her head and that she would not have believed it if it had. (One day

Mammy was to ride with me in my own plane, but that was to be as far in the future as it is now in the past.)

Except as forced punishment which we could not evade, we were not given to staying indoors, carriage shed or elsewhere. We hadn't been caught at anything for several gratifying days, and Mother became a little curious as she heard us hammering away in the shed from sunup to sundown. We walked into the house one evening and she asked us what we were building. We replied truthfully enough—an airplane. I don't recall just what she was doing at the time, but she kept right on for several moments, then stopped, looked down at Bill and asked, "Did you say an airplane?" He looked up at her with steady, open affection as I have seen him do a thousand times and replied, "Yes'm." Mother was never enchanted by aircraft to the slightest degree, which was fortunate for us because the thought never occurred to her to ask what we proposed to do with it after we finished it. But, in a sense, it wasn't so fortunate for me, for here was a chance to get out of the pilot's job once and for all. I needed only to speak; but while I might have stood for Mother to see how scared I was, I could not parade my fright before the others, so I said nothing.

The construction of our plane went on apace until it was finally completed to the last rusty nail, twisted piece of baling wire, and soiled grocery sack. Dudley, a handyman about the place, was called to lend a hand and we all got set to push it out of the shed and into the light of a bright summer day, only to discover that the door of the shed was too narrow for the long, single wing. While we were wondering why Bill had not long ago come up with some figures by which we could have been spared this state of affairs, he was busy instructing us to knock the wing loose from the frame so we could push the sections out of the door one at a time. Our good will toward the job had been punctured, and our faith in Bill's overall capacity as designing and construction engineer had been appreciably lessened. On the other hand, we couldn't see any way to avoid having to follow his new orders; after all we were not unionized and thus had little access to a bargaining table, and besides he was the biggest. Though our hearts were no longer totally in the task, we took up our tools and set to work disengaging the wing from the frame. During the process several of the partially rotten planks gave up and fell apart, but we succeeded in shoving the whole machine out into the lot, where we rebuilt the wing and again nailed it to the frame.

Bill had already selected the site for the takeoff. It was the edge of the deepest ditch at the far end of the pasture below the barn. I knew it well and had found it a delightful place to scramble up and down, but that was before I had been informed that I was to be shoved off the edge of it. In the carefree days before I became a pilot it had struck me as being shallow, but the more I thought of it, the deeper it got, and I began to doubt that I had ever been able to see the bottom from any conceivable vantage point. My misgivings were not calmed very much by Bill's explanation that we would drag and shove the machine to the ditch, then set it right on the edge; I would take my place on the pilot's two by four, and nothing would remain but for the crew to shove me and the plane smartly over the edge.

While the others, including Dudley, were overflowing with excitement and anticipation, I would have been shaking in my shoes had I not already discarded them to save weight. And if I had the slightest doubt as to what the immediate future likely held for me, it was promptly dissipated when I crawled onto the pilot's plank, took a glimpse at the apparently bottomless abyss below as the machine rested precariously on the edge of it, and awaited the cheerful shove of my fellow aeronauts.

When everything seemed to be ready, including me, trembling on the frail plank in the no-bottom cabin, everyone took a deep breath and Bill yelled, "Shove!" But nothing happened. The combined force of the pushers was insufficient to budge the contraption. This meant that more pushing power was needed and, while I realized that I was too scared to have much strength left, I was ready and anxious to offer it in such a worthy cause. Besides, this would get me out of the pilot's seat. I was surprised how quickly my strength surged within me, for I popped out of the compartment, taking two of the three starboard slats with me, ducked under the wing and planted myself at the extreme end of the tail section before the others knew what was happening. Sallie Murry and John were already there pushing and heaving, and there wasn't much more room for another, even one with such willing hands as mine.

John was ready to try anything once, or oftener if the notion struck him. As I tried to nudge in between him and Sallie, he was struck by one which I could find no reason to object to. He withdrew from his stand, trotted around to the front, and called to Bill that I should take his place because I could push harder, and he would take the pilot's seat because he was lighter. But Bill, our crew chief in word and deed, would have none of the suggestion, saying that it was going to take the shoving of all of us to get the machine off. Together we heaved, and then there was a sudden thump as the undercarriage plopped down into a small hole between the hump and the edge of the ditch. Now, we quickly found, we were worse off than ever, for we would not only have to push but lift and shove at the same time. Bill moved around to the front of the craft and surveyed the unpromising situation. He

then set Dudley on one side, me on the other, and Sallie
Murry and John at the back, saying that when he gave the
word we were to all lift and push until he called stop.

Since Bill had stationed himself at the front, his back was
to the ditch and he was thus pulling as the rest of us lifted
and pushed. He gave the word, we all gave a mighty heave,
and the plane suddenly reared its tail like a lively pony and
seemed to bounce out of the depression. Bill had to jump
aside to keep from being shoved into the ditch by the nose
which was now tottering on the very edge of the precipice. In
a few pulsating seconds things had changed and now anyone
could plainly see that we were on the verge of the first manned
flight in the state of Mississippi. But we had to hurry, and Bill
did not hesitate. He shouted that he was the nearest one to
the pilot's plank, would take over, and for us to hang on to
the plane until he got set. There was nothing we could do or
say; after all, it was, in effect, his airplane. He squirmed into
the pilot's cage, grasped the stays by which it was nailed to
the wing and shouted, "Let go!"

We jerked our hands away, the tail bounded skyward, and
it hung on the edge for a second, then commenced a slow
backhand drop. I suppose that a pilot twenty years later
would have called it a tail-first inverted loop, provided a real
plane could be made to execute such an implausible maneuver. But whatever it could be called, on that bright day in
a Mississippi back pasture more than a half century ago, it was
not very violent and did not last very long. The machine
never actually got away from the red clay side of the ditch
as it skidded gently down to the white sand at the bottom,
shedding the while rusty nails, old grocery sacks, rotten
planks, and pilot. Bill was barely scratched, not even enough
to leave any lasting memento of the first man (or child) to
become airborne in Mississippi—well, almost.

5 THE COLONEL AND HIS BUICK

THE COMING OF THE AUTOMOBILE BROUGHT SOME CHANGES to Oxford, and not necessarily for the better. It pushed back horizons and made people impatient to get to them. When the first cars came to town, gasoline and oil were sold from drums in the hardware stores (we had never heard of a filling station), and since there was but one grade of each, every motorist got the same thing. It was amazing to see the transformation in a man whose trusted horse had a top speed of perhaps eight miles an hour, and who had taken a week or a month to even consider when he was going to travel, let alone where. When this same man acquired his first automobile, he immediately set out to run roughshod over everyone in sight in an effort to get under way within the hour.

Grandfather bought one of the first automobiles in town, notwithstanding the fact that he himself had seen to it that an ordinance was passed the previous year forbidding the operation of one within the town limits. It was a 1909 model Buick touring car, no doors in front, a rubber bulb horn attached to the steering wheel column, brass trimmings all over, right-hand drive, gasoline and spark levers on a quadrant above the steering wheel, completely smooth no-tread tires, carbide lights, big gear shift, and hand brake levers offset on a heavy rod extending out from the right front floor board. The motor could be started by an ingenious device known as a hand crank, but whether it worked at any given time or not depended equally upon the strength and persistence of the cranker and the current temperament of the motor.

The lights were gas burners, fed by a double-section, pure brass, vertical cylinder rigidly attached to the right running board. The lower section held carbide, purchased at the drugstore, while the upper was the water container, to which there was fixed a little regulating valve to determine the amount of water allowed to drip down onto the carbide, which, of course, controlled the size of the small flames in the V-burners in each of the big headlights. It took an intrepid soul to travel by night in a car in those days, but, then, for that matter, it took such a one to buy an automobile in the first place. When a ride by night was contemplated the car was first driven to a wide open space, of which Oxford had plenty in those far-off times. This was advisable (a mild word indeed) because when the valve was turned on the carbide unit, one never knew whether the gas would flow through the brass feed pipes to the headlights with a gentle hiss or whether the whole outfit would blow up in one's face.

Now that the Colonel had his automobile, someone was needed to drive it. He selected Chess, a colored man who worked for the family on and off at the home place or the bank, the latter having been established by Grandfather and some friends in 1910 with himself as its first president. Naturally Chess did not know how to drive an automobile. One might say that this was only a small drawback, seeing that all he had to do was to take a few driving lessons, but it wasn't that easy. To begin with, no one in town had ever driven a car and few had ever been inside one. It was to Chess's eternal credit that he had sufficient native ingenuity, perseverance, and imagination (plus, perhaps, a disinclination to cross the Colonel) that he was able to overcome every obstacle and teach himself to operate a machine he had never seen before, with all its gadgets, knobs, levers, pedals, and switches. In the process, he also taught himself to be an expert mechanic, although this was probably an acquired defense against a machine as perverse as the Buick. Its slick tires lasted not over a few hundred miles, and it took the combined efforts of everyone in the neighborhood to get one on or off a rim; the valves had to be reground and reset, carbon cleaned out, and the entire ignition system worked over completely after about two hundred miles of operation.

Colonel had an old harness house near the barn converted into a garage for the car. It was set up about six feet off the ground, and when it was made into a garage it was necessary to remove the entry ladder and construct a ramp in its place, in order that the car could be driven up and into the building. The barnyard was entered from the back street by driving through a sort of hallway in the barn; then a ninety-degree left turn had to be made to face the ramp, but it was too steep, because the Buick motor, big though it was in size, was too lacking in power to enable the car to climb up the ramp from a standing start at the bottom. This meant that it was necessary to back the car against the south fence, then take a running start and hit the ramp wide open. The garage itself was just barely long and wide enough to contain the car, so getting up and into its narrow confines was truly a ticklish business. One had to get enough speed between the fence and the ramp for the momentum of the car to rocket it up the ramp, then, at the precise instant that the rear wheels cleared the top, full brakes had to be applied instantaneously to keep the hurtling car from flying through the rear wall of the garage.

I found that automobiles held a great fascination for me as a boy, as airplanes did in later life. Colonel let me learn to drive the Buick on instructions grudgingly given by Chess. It naturally followed that I soon became convinced that I too could put the car in the garage. Late one afternoon Colonel and Bill and I went to the barnyard with Chess in the car and again I asked to be allowed to drive it in. Colonel must have become tired of refusing, for this time he told Chess to back the car against the lower fence and let me take over. I must have been about twelve or thirteen—and barely big enough to see over the dashboard.

It took all my strength to depress the clutch and the fullest extent of my reaching to stretch out and shove the gear shift into the low speed notch. By this time the back of my neck was shoved against the seat. As I had seen Chess do many times, I tugged the gasoline lever all the way down on the quadrant. The motor roared, the car shook, and yellow flames spewed out from the open exhaust. I cast a quick glance at the Colonel, Chess, and Bill standing safely away from the boiling, bucking Buick. They were—in order—apprehensive, angry, and delighted. I then peeked over the dashboard for a good look to line up the big radiator snout with the ramp and jerked my foot off the clutch pedal. The Buick shot out across the yard like a suddenly uncaged rabbit. I juggled with the steering wheel, keeping the radiator snout lined up on the center of the ramp, which I had to hit no matter what. I did, with a bang that could have been heard in the next county, but I was too intent with the steering wheel to think of the gasoline lever, much less to stamp down on the brakes. When I thought of them a second later it was too late to avoid disaster. The Buick roared up the ramp at such an angle that the front part kept right on going and for a split second I felt certain that the car was going to hang itself on a rafter. I was frozen into immobility, scared almost out of my wits; the gasoline lever remained wide open and I could not have found the brake pedal with a dozen feet. With scantlings, sheared-off posts, and rusty nails flying about my ears, we tore through the back wall of the building and leaped about twenty feet through the air, then plunked down into the soft and welcome earth of the freshly tilled garden. It was a mess; it was also many a day before the Colonel turned me loose again to put the car in the garage.

One day the Colonel had invited some friends to go for an evening ride and told Chess to come for him at the Opera House. I was asked to ride that far to help in getting the headlights lit. The Opera House was on the square, set back a little from the street which, as events turned out, was not far enough. After making a grand and imposing halt in front of the place, Chess descended on his side, stood beside the double-decked, brass carbide gas generator and waited while I went around to the front of the car and got out a big kitchen match. I struck it and waited for word from him when to apply the flame to the V-shaped gas jets in each lamp. He cautiously opened the drip valve lever and we listened closely, hearing no hiss and smelling no odor to indicate (as was frequently the case) that the gas was escaping elsewhere. He opened the valve wider and I leaned over until my head was almost in one of the headlights. At that instant the brass cylinder exploded, rocking Chess and me on our heels. I grabbed the radiator to steady myself and looked at Chess. His big-brimmed straw hat was circled with small, vicious flames and he was staring up at the second story of the Opera House. While we had been trying to get the lights fired up, Mr. Ben Conley, the owner of the House, and a friend were standing at the only window on the second floor, fascinated by the possibility of soon seeing the lights on the town's one and only automobile flash up in all their brilliance. They seemed brilliant in those days of oil lamps and gas lights, although it is doubtful if the cantankerous carbide gas lights, even when they would work for as much as ten minutes at a stretch, could produce more than a generous top of twenty-five candlepower. Anyway, as the two were watching Chess and me prepare the Buick for the night excursion, their guardian angels had not forsaken them. Mr. Conley told me later that the window wouldn't open and they stepped back into the room looking for something to use to pry it open. At the instant they left the window the brass top of the gas generator blasted through the pane, slammed against the wall, bounced off the ceiling, and crashed down at Mr. Conley's feet.

I jerked my now blistered hand away from the boiling hot radiator and looked at Chess again. His beard was singed completely off one side of his face, an entire sleeve had been blasted away at his shoulder, and all that was left of his hat was a neat little pile of charred fragments on the ground beside him.

On another occasion, so the story goes, the Colonel had attended a convention in Jackson, the capital. Having gotten word of the hour of his return, Chess met his train in Oxford. Grandfather and some of his cronies had been on the train for a sufficient number of hours to imbibe a fair amount of exhilarating spirits. All were happy and filled with good

cheer when they descended from the train to get into the car.
There were not many places where a car could be driven in
Oxford then, and fewer still where such animated passengers would consent to be driven. This so narrowed the choice
that soon Chess was driving around and around the square.
After several cheerful circles had been negotiated, the Colonel ordered Chess to stop, get out, and pick up a brick lying
beside the board walk. The Colonel took the brick and told
Chess to drive slowly by the bank, broadside on. It was near-
ing nightfall and bank employees had long since departed
and locked up for the night. Moreover, the bank had the biggest plate glass window in town, and a glance was all that was
needed to confirm that the place was indeed deserted. By
this time the Buick's motor had become overheated and a
full-bodied stream of vapor was pouring out of the snout,
like a freight engine going uphill on a cold winter day. As
the car steamed slowly past the bank, the Colonel stood up,
steadied himself on the back of the front seat, took careful
aim amid the cheers of his comrades, and heaved the brick.
Under the circumstances, his aim was surprisingly accurate.
A well-placed stick of dynamite could not have ripped out
the window more completely. Later that evening, the Colonel
was still taking a nip now and then, totally unencumbered by
any feeling of remorse. When someone asked him why he
heaved the brick, his answer, entirely in keeping with the
logic of the occasion was, "It was my Buick, my brick, and
my bank."

The Colonel had a big office at the rear of the bank and in
it was a great roll-top desk of pure mahogany so littered and
stacked with papers and pamphlets that the top could not
have been lowered even if he ever had a notion to bother
with it. There were also several tremendous leather chairs
of the period and probably what was the last real, bed-size

leather couch ever manufactured. He used to say that only the foolish or unfortunate would contend with the midday sun. He evidently considered himself in neither of these categories, as he always had Chess drive him home promptly at noon for dinner, not lunch. The latter, to him, meant food unworthy of serious consideration, such as lemonade and lady fingers, both of which he abhorred.

Immediately following this expansive repast he would either retire to his bedroom or return to his office for a long nap. If he elected to remain at home, he could depend on Auntee to see to it that he was not disturbed. The office presented a somewhat different problem, though the result was identical. If he returned to his office, he had Chess draw one of the big chairs to the door and carefully set it directly in the center. Then Chess would seat himself in it as a guard, to make certain that the Colonel's nap was not interrupted by some fool with an outrageous idea of transacting some trifling legal or banking business during the heat of the day. Chess was no fool, and he had served the Colonel so long that he probably knew as much about him as the Colonel knew about himself. Perhaps even more, for on the reasonable ground that what may be beneficial for one may be equally so for another, Chess contrived to take his restful nap in the chair while the Colonel was sleeping on the sofa, which meant that Chess must have developed some sort of perception by which he could bring himself to wakefulness a few seconds before the Colonel. And it never failed him.

I remember one trip we made to Memphis with the Colonel. There were, in addition to Chess and the Colonel, Auntee, Sallie Murry, Bill, and me. All roads were dirt then, and it usually took the better part of a full day to get there, depending on the weather, the car, the Colonel's temper, and how many cattle we encountered on the road. When we hit one, and we hit many, it immediately became the top specimen in the aristocracy of cattledom.

Preparing to go to Memphis in a car then was roughly equivalent to preparing for a trip to Mars today. Before a bag was packed, the Buick had to be stored with extra tires and tubes, tire patches, a big hand pump, several pieces of long rope, chains for all four wheels, a lantern, a hammer, a hatchet, and extra cans of gasoline and oil. One did not specify any particular type of gasoline or oil, since all came in bulk and were different only to the extent that one went into the motor by way of the carburetor and the other through the oil spout.

We prepared to start out literally at the crack of day, and it would be a long day, especially for the Colonel who, on orders from Auntee (since the death of Granny he would accept none from anyone else), would have to forego his "chawing" tobacco for a full day. On rides about Oxford he always sat in the back seat, but on cross-country trips he would usually sit in front beside Chess so he could better see what was going on and be in a position to issue driving instructions when he felt they were needed. No matter how many he gave, Chess always contrived to keep right on driving just as he intended doing in the first place.

Our big basket containing lunch and dinner had been carefully placed on the front seat between the Colonel and Chess; tire chains and what-not had been accounted for; a good portion of the family had gathered in the faint light of early dawn to see us off; the motor had been cranked and our spirits soared with exhilaration and unrestrained anticipation. With an expert and meaningful gesture Chess reached proudly for the big brass gearshift lever and at that precise instant the heretofore completely sound right front tire blew out with a bang that woke all the neighbors who were not already abroad to see us set out. When the tire exploded the Buick shifted abruptly to starboard and shifted Grandfather onto the dinner basket, and his alpaca-coated right elbow dug into a segment of his favorite apple pie. We had been with him often enough to recognize the symptoms and we knew what to expect now, but this time Auntee was within arm's length. Grandfather's face took on the reddish hue of pre-explosion anger, his linen tourist cap trembled on his head, and he was just about to blow up like the tire, when Auntee reached over, touched him gently on the arm, and said, "Now Pappy, don't."

By now a number of folks were about, silently regarding the tilted Buick and its passengers. Not one evidenced any overwhelming inclination to wrestle with a flat tire at four-thirty in the morning, well knowing, as all did, that once such a finger-cracking, back-breaking job was begun it was certain to defy completion for at least two or three hours, and only an unrestrained fool would set out for Memphis as late as seven or eight o'clock in the morning.

The next day things went better. We actually did get under way at the crack of dawn. Well before sunup we had arrived at the long sand bed near College Hill, a good four miles from town. The ruts were deep, the treadless tires were slick, the sand was fine, and Chess decided to make a run at it, which meant putting the car in second gear, then building up to a good, flying start before hitting the sand, with the hope that the speed of the car on entry would be sufficient to keep up momentum and enable it to plow through the deep sand onto solid ground beyond in one mighty and irresistible surge. It didn't work and I don't suppose any of us really believed that it would. We wound up in the middle of the deepest section of the sand and settled down with a jolt up to the running boards.

We used to wonder how word could get ahead of us so

quickly that we had started out for Memphis, were about
to, or soon would. At any rate, before Chess could shut off
the motor up came two citizens of the community driving
two sullen mules to which was attached a relatively new chain
just right to fit a 1909 Buick touring car. Under similar circumstances on earlier trips, when Auntee was not present,
Colonel had blown his top, and if our tender ears had heard
some choice cuss words, we could at least say that they had
been uttered by a master. But now Auntee was with us, and
no doubt Grandfather realized the futility of telling the two
bland and uninspiring drivers to their greedy faces that they
had dug the ruts deeper, harnessed their mules, and hid out
in the brush just waiting for us to come along. No matter
now, one way or the other the Colonel had to pay to get out:
they knew it and he knew it. Neither the men nor the mules
glanced at us or the car. They came up beside it and one of
the men scratched the back of his neck, pushed the other,
younger, one toward the car, then, as though addressing the
empty woods, the red sand, or even the mules, said, "That'll
be three dollars." The last time it had been only two and the
Colonel's face began to get red again. But once more Auntee
quickly reached over, touched him gently on the arm, and
repeated, "Now Pappy, don't."

Five blowouts, three more towouts, and fourteen hours
later we arrived in Memphis—but still short of our final destination, the Peabody Hotel, then on Main Street. We could
see the hard-surface street ahead as we toiled through the
last stretch of the rutted surface over which we had labored
the live-long day. Now anticipation of better things to come
took hold; surely we would soon be rolling smartly along the
fine hard-topped road at twenty-five or maybe even thirty
miles an hour. Surely now, we thought, our troubles of the
day were behind us and ahead was a speedy, exhilarating
ride to Main Street.

The weather had been clear and pleasant all day, and we had been too busy after nightfall fixing two punctures and nursing the headlights to notice the black clouds now hovering overhead. One might have said with considerable justification that the weatherman had been keeping a mean and cunning eye on us ever since we left Oxford in preparation for the torrential deluge that engulfed us precisely as we drove onto the hard-top road. The Buick promptly skidded across the slick surface and into a small depression on the far side. It took us about thirty minutes to raise the cloth top, by which time we were all as wet as if we had jumped into the Mississippi, and the puddles were as numerous inside the car as out. I do not know exactly what proportion of water to carbide was needed to keep the headlights burning, but whatever it was, it now became too much and the dim, flickering flames in the V-burners finally gave a feeble quiver and died completely.

Here we were, after approximately fifteen hours of some riding, much pushing, and an inordinate amount of pumping, almost within sight of the hotel and, with no chains on the treadless tires for traction, we could not move an inch. Much sweat and an almost complete disdain for danger was needed to crank a horseless carriage; all of this, plus about three hours of incessant manual labor, was needed to change a tire—as hard and exasperating as any human labor could be.

But to put chains on the tires—ah, to put chains on the tires. It weakens me even now to think about it. First, they had to be taken out of one of the big tool boxes on the running board, where they were invariably at the bottom (and everything else was spilled out in the process of getting at them); then the jack had to be fished out of another tool box on the other running board. Then, with jack and operating handle in hand, one had to lie down on his back and shove with his heels to push himself up under the car to put

the jack under the axle. The man with the jack under the car
was then entirely on his own, with a little six-inch handle to
actuate it, his grit, and his God—and he needed them all.
Finally the tire cleared the ground and the real work began,
for all the passengers in the car and for any passerby who
could be enticed, cajoled, or frightened into lending a hand.

The chains had hooks on one end and clasps on the other
end, useful only if and when they could ever be made to
meet. The opening move would be to drape the chain carefully and precisely over the tire; the next would be to note
with consternation and despair that, no matter how tight it
was pressed on the tire, it always lacked three or four inches
of meeting clasp to hook.

We wrestled with the chains in the downpour; Auntee
held the lantern, the Colonel and Bill tugged at the end with
the hook, while Chess and I heaved and puffed with the
clasp. We were in Memphis all right, but we could not have
been more dependent on our own feeble efforts had we been
in the middle of an otherwise deserted island. Finally Bill
and Chess were stretched out flat on the street, one pushing
and the other pulling at the hook, while the Colonel and I
were on our knees pushing and shoving at the clasp—but still
they would not meet. Maybe because she was not busy and
could think, or maybe just because she was a woman, Auntee
was the first to have enough of the back-breaking comedy,
and she dared voice an alternative to put an end to it. Her
suggestion was at once simple, direct—and outrageous, "Let
some air out of the tires so the chain ends can be forced together and locked."

It should be understood by the reader that a ride in any
automobile in 1910 was, in effect, a succession of punctures
and blowouts, with all the toil and frustration that each
brought. When one, then, was faced with such an incredible
alternative as voluntarily letting air out of tires that were so

Photograph taken at John Faulkner's home in Oxford about 1940 shows
John standing in the back row with his wife Lucille at his right and his
brother Dean's widow Louise at his left; second row, seated left to right,
the Fa(u)lkner boys' Auntee, their mother, their Uncle John Falkner and
Aunt Sue; front row, another generation of Falkners—Chooky, Dean, and
Jimmy.

Home of Colonel J. W. T. Falkner on South Street, Oxford, Mississippi. The Colonel was the grandfather of William, Murry, John, and Dean.

Colonel J. W. T. Falkner

Sallie Murry Falkner (Granny)

Colonel Falkner and his Buick in a mud hole near Oxford about 1910.
The man seated on the fender of the car is unidentified.

The Falkner brothers, about 1910. William, the oldest, stands between Murry (to his right) and John. The youngest is Dean.

SALLIE MURRY WILLIAMS

William strums a guitar in this snap-
shot taken at Oxford about 1914.

Dean Falkner as a small boy.

Christmas 1929

Dear Dean,

There was a man in the office this morning said he
saw a bird pass Abbeville that had never been shot at, by you,
The bird asked the man where he thought he would be safe, and
the man told him to go to Hell.

Love   DAD

M. C. FALKNER, Sect. & Bus-Mgr.

LOUISE FAULKNER MEADOW

Note which the Falkner boys' father wrote his son Dean reveals humorous
side of the man. The father and son hunted together.

William Faulkner beside his Waco 210 Continental at Oxford, 1933. This is the plane in which, two years later, his brother Dean was killed.

Murry Falkner in his Aeronca at the Dean Falkner Memorial Airport near Oxford, prior to takeoff for San Francisco, May, 1939.

Murry Falkner with FBI Director J. Edgar Hoover, Roswell, New Mexico, 1937.

John Faulkner in pilot's uniform about 1939.

Pilot identification card issued to Dean Faulkner in October, 1934, a few months before his death in a plane crash near Pontotoc, Mississippi.

Top left, the Falkner boys' Auntee and their cousin Sallie Murry, about 1940. Top right, Murry Falkner's wife Suzanne, whom he met and married in North Africa. Bottom, Maud Butler Falkner, mother of William, Murry, John, and Dean—Oxford, 1945.

monstrously difficult to keep air in, one could say that only a fool would even think of it. Moreover, tires in those days were far more delicate in posture than the most conscientiously baked upside-down cake and much more likely to collapse at the least provocation, which meant that if one dared to test this tender balance by letting out, say, ten pounds of air, it could virtually be taken as a foregone conclusion that he would end up in a poof with none at all. The Colonel, of course, had to make the dreadful decision. Chess, who often read the latter's thoughts before he had time to express them, was already on his feet and getting the big black pump out when Grandfather raised himself to a standing position, wiped the rain from his eyes with a raw and greasy hand, helped Bill and me to our feet, gave the rear fender a swift, solid kick, and said, "Dammit—deflate 'em!"

Chains were put on tires as a last extremity, as an act by its very nature so potent with calamity that circumstances would admit of no other, as a final admission of total and irrevocable abandonment by fate, guardian angel, and fellow man. It would seem quite reasonable to suppose that after all the mortal stress and strain needed to get the clasps into the hooks there could not possibly be any free play whatever between chain and tire; yet, with the first revolution of the wheel, the unending banging of chain against fender would begin. If chains had to be put on all four wheels, the banging was never in unison, because the chain on each wheel would blast against the underside of each fender in perfect and earsplitting rotation—left rear, right front, left front, right rear, continuously, heedlessly, and spitefully. It may well be that there was some precise physical law governing what happened when chains were placed on 1909 model automobiles, but whatever it was, it was invisible to the human eye and incomprehensible to the human mind.

With but one jack, only one wheel could be raised at a

time, and the Colonel and Chess decided that we could probably finish the trip if chains were put just on the rear wheels. Bill was allowed to push the valve in gently to let some air out of one tire, and I got the same job for the other. Perhaps they figured that the cantankerous tires would take it as less of an affront if manipulated solely by children. Miraculously enough, it worked; then all we had to do was to pump up the tires again.

Even in the innocent and uncluttered year of 1910 an automobile tour could be made without many things, but a pump was not one of them. It was as essential as the motor and wheels and sometimes was used more frequently than either. Pumps of that day had a stroke of about twenty inches when new. The one in the Buick had been used untold times; therefore, the washers in the cylinder were so worn that they would force air through the pump tube and into the tires only during the last two or three inches of the stroke. Its spirit was weak, and, soon enough, so were ours, as well as our arms, legs, and backs, but we persisted out of pure desperation and simple necessity. After about two hours the second of the two tires had been pumped anew with good, fresh Tennessee air. Again Chess crawled up under the car and lowered the wheels. At that exact instant, as suddenly as it had begun, the rain stopped. I looked at the heavens and never saw a clearer sky. I looked at the blacktop and saw that the retained heat of a long, summer day was already beginning to dry it. Now, of course, we didn't need the chains; indeed, without appreciable moisture on the street, they would be almost certain to rip the tires to shreds before we had gone a block.

Auntee was hardly a lantern-carrying lady, nor was Grandfather, in truth, a tire-fixing man. Now each had had enough of the perversity of fate, automobile, and weather. Without saying a word, Auntee herded Sallie Murry and Bill and me back into the car, took her place, and looked at the Colonel. He glanced at her, then turned his head and nodded at Chess and stepped up into the front seat. Chess put the tools away, turned on the ignition switch, set the gas and spark levers, went to the crank, hesitated a moment as he looked at the Colonel, and asked, "We'se gwine now—wid dem chains to sholy rip up de tiahs?"

"We are," repiled Grandfather, "if we have to drive up to the Peabody on the rims."

6 "ME AND ED AND JIM WILL TAKE ON THE FALKNER BOYS"

OXFORD WAS ON A BRANCH LINE OF THE ILLINOIS CEN-
tral railroad extending from Grenada, Mississippi, to
Paducah, Kentucky, and it was a busy line during the years
when we were growing up. There were four passenger trains
each way every day and two local freights, plus many through-
freights day and night. As far as the male population of the
town was concerned, the railroad station was a sort of focal
point. Most men and nearly all the boys found time to go
there frequently and watch the trains go by.

Every engineer had his own assigned locomotive and his
own distinctive touch to the beautiful whistle on it; and we
knew them all, by sight and sound. Often we could hear one

laboring up Thacker's Mountain (elevation about three hundred feet) seven miles south of town. Then, as it began the gentle descent to the level track leading into town, its exhaust would quicken to a rapid beat and we knew that the soul-lilting wail of the whistle would quickly follow. As soon as we heard it we could declare without possibility of error, for instance, "That's Mr. Markette with number 849," or "That's Mr. McLeod with number 912," and we were never mistaken—as I say, we knew them all.

What we called the "fruit trains" would begin running through Oxford in the latter part of February or early March each year. These were trains taking the strawberry crop from southern Mississippi and Louisiana to the northern market, and they carried it in a hurry: even the regular passenger trains were sometimes set out on sidetracks to let the fruit trains thunder by. The time of their departure from the fruit-producing areas put the first ones through Oxford at about five o'clock in the morning, and Bill, John, and I would scurry down to the railroad to watch them almost every day. The best vantage point was the high bank on the University side of the tracks south of the station.

Frequently day was just beginning to break as we got ourselves settled to enjoy what was, to us, the most fascinating and entertaining show on earth. Had we a fortune, we would gladly have given it for what we were getting free. Soon we would hear the distant and wonderful whistle of the first locomotive as it cleared Thacker's Mountain. The soft, gentle air of the serene countryside brought the heart-stirring sound to three boys sitting in a row on the dewy bank high above the track—"Whoo-oo, whoo-ah, whoo-oo, whoo-oo, whoo-ah-ah-ah." As the train entered the level straightaway track south of town we could plainly hear the quickening of the locomotive's exhaust—at first heavy and dull, then (as the speed increased) light, sharp, precise, and distinct. When it had regained almost full speed on the level track, the wheels hummed on the rails, and the exhaust beats were so rapid that one was barely out of the stack before another exploded upon it—and again the magnificent whistle spilled and spread out its song upon the quiet countryside, at once lonely, lovely, and unforgettable.

Now the wonderful locomotive pounds into view, the red glare from the open firebox door quivering against the underside of the exhaust smoke column swirling almost flat above the cab and tender, and we arise as one to get even a better view. It is still too distant for us to make out the number on the giant of the rails, but the whistle has already identified it for us. Bill says what we are waiting to hear, though in truth we know it as well as he, "That's Mr. Smith in number 1031." And, of course, he is right.

I would hesitate to say that it was done just to confuse us, but once in a while, for some reason or other, a different engineer would be on an engine usually assigned to another. But even that didn't present us with any identification problem; we knew that a different hand was pulling the whistle cord.

Until vacation time Mother insisted that we get back home from train-watching in time to eat breakfast and then go on to school. We always made it, although it was heartrending business to leave when we knew that another fine locomotive would be along in a little while. Conditions were happily different when the fruit-train season ran on into the summer months, as it sometimes did, for then we could devote the entire day to train-watching, or at least for as long as the trains ran, and this went on until late afternoon when the empty ones came back south again. During especially busy periods, the railroad would put into use every locomo-

tive which could carry a head of steam, from tiny fifty-inch
drive wheel switch engines to big, beautiful ten and eleven
hundred class passenger locomotives. The latter were designed to generate considerable speed, with their long-stroke
pistons and seventy-two-inch drive wheels, whereas the little
ones were barely capable of hauling half the tonnage at half
the speed.

With spring then, as now, came baseball, but no single
nine-inning game was enough for us; when one ended we
would "choose up" and start all over again. We usually played
in our side yard and, generally, each boy played the position
that best suited his natural ability, determination, and instant
willingness to take on anyone who thought he could do a
better job. Bill was the pitcher, John the shortstop, and I
ended up as catcher, largely because no one else wanted that
back- and finger-breaking task; thus I didn't have to fight or
even argue to hold it. For the most part the other players
were of our age group, but not infrequently older boys and
even some grown men would join in the fun. The men evidently found it both simple and convenient to get away from
their labors in town and join in during the late hours of the
long summer afternoons. They would arrive singly or in
groups and watch us scampering about our improvised diamond as they shed their ties and rolled up their sleeves. Then
Mr. Neilson would call out, "Me and Ed and Jim will take
on the Falkner boys!" I suppose he named us directly because
we were always there. Moreover, it was our yard. What he
actually meant was that now some grownups would be on
each nine-man or -boy team.

It didn't take me long to discover that the men could tip
a ball farther and harder backward than we could paste it
with all our might in front. This meant that by the second

or third inning I had gradually backed all the way to the barn fence. Anyone could steal second then, or any other base for that matter, if I were depended on to throw him out, for from where I had then carefully positioned myself I could barely throw the ball back to home plate, much less to the bases out beyond it. Somehow or other, though, we would finally manage to get the other side out, and then came our turn at bat. It isn't easy for a boy to hit a ball thrown by someone twice his size and strength, but we did our best, neither asking nor expecting favors of anyone. John was the best of us, being able, with remarkable frequency, to belt the ball clean out of the yard on the fly. He had much natural athletic ability, and went on to play shortstop and quarterback throughout high school and college.

One day in a memorable game (because the Falkner boys and their "side" had actually tied the score, 21 to 21 or 37 to 37, give or take a few runs) the opposition came to bat after we had pushed across twelve or fifteen sweet and sweaty runs. Mr. Neilson came to bat, the bases were loaded, the kind and gentle Mrs. Bell was quietly reading her Bible in her upstairs bedroom in the house across the street, I had backed all the way to the barn fence (and would have been crouched behind it except for my pride), and Bill prepared to deliver the first pitch. He had to do this entirely on his own, for even if I had not already completely run out of ideas as to what Mr. Neilson could not hit, I was so far away from the pitcher's mound that Bill would have needed a spyglass to see what signal my grimy figures could concoct.

Hoping against hope that Mr. Neilson could be held to a double or triple rather than a base-unloading home run, we grimly awaited Bill's delivery. He made a noble effort, winding up wide, handsome, and all over just like he had been trying to teach John and me for weeks. His right-leg knicker had already pulled apart and was draped about his leg. Now the other one popped loose, too, and when he unwound, his baseball cap flew off as he let go with as mighty a heave as a twelve-year-old boy could. Unhappily, no matter how fast it was by our standards, it was well within Mr. Neilson's capacity to judge and swat. His bat met the ball with a crack which could be heard down on the square, and the ball took off on a towering trajectory across the diamond, over the fence, above the trees in front of Mrs. Bell's house, and right through her second-story window with a shattering of glass.

As may be the general rule, those fine souls who read the Bible most may well be the ones who need it least. Certain it is that Mrs. Bell's ever-forgiving and always considerate character had been formed long before this pleasant summer afternoon when a fifteen-cent baseball shattered her windowpane, bounced off her wall, dropped onto her mantel, and then plopped down onto her open Bible in her lap. She told us later that it didn't even make her lose her place.

My brothers and I were, by and large, sufficient unto ourselves, in the sense that we had no bosom friends. We were far from being alone with ourselves, though; we played games and hunted with boys of our age and attended many social affairs with the girls. In the summer we would gather on the front porch at the home of a girl and dance to music from a Gramophone or played by the girl at the family piano. Bill was of fine figure, liked to dress well, was an excellent dancer, and was much in demand by the girls as a dancing partner. John was all of that, plus being one of the two handsomest boys in town. I impressed few, including myself, very much or very long.

As we grew into our teens, Mother continued to instill in us a love for the printed word. Some of what we read was directly connected with our school work; some we read on suggestions from Mother, though she preferred that our own curiosity about our world lead us to books and subjects of our own choosing. On the other hand, none of us ever became a "bookworm." Bill and John, and later Dean in his time, made excellent grades in school with so little effort that on several occasions each was "skipped" a grade, having completed two years of school work in one. I did well to hold my own. Bill read almost everything he could get his hands on, but had little truck with school after reaching fifteen or so.

Dean was considerably younger than the rest of us, which meant that his boyhood was spent not with his brothers but with boys of his own age. He was also the last to be in Mammy's charge, and she relinquished some measure of it only with the utmost reluctance. When he passed from babyhood there was no one left in the family for Mammy to nurse, unless she could figure out some way to keep him under her wing, school or no school. She was not one to give up easily, and her ingenuity did not fail even with the passing of time. At the age of seven he entered school, and in her seventies so did Mammy. As a member of the family, she was expected to explain any questionable actions only when called upon to do so by Father or Mother, which the latter did when it was discovered that Mammy was accompanying Dean to school each day. Mother patiently explained that Dean was no longer a baby, did not need to be looked after all day, and must be allowed to get along without her.

The next day Mammy was up bright and early again. She could be, since all she had to do was to wake up. She had her own table in the kitchen, and the cook served her just as she did the rest of us (actually quicker, because Mammy was there in the kitchen where the meal was being prepared). But this time she hurried (she could eat almost as many hot biscuits

with ham gravy as I could) and went out the back door, around
the yard, and down the street a block, where she waited for
Dean to come by on his way to school. This went on for
several days before Mother found out about it. I don't recall
what trifling event exposed Mammy. Under the ordinary
course of events she might have continued going to school
with him for an indefinite period because, aside from looking after the household as she had for years, she now had no
specific duties assigned to her and was thus free to come and
go. Of course, in a sense, she was now actually going to school,
too, for she was spending as much time on the school premises
as Dean, but with the advantage of not having to listen to
someone expounding on some set subjects. Thus she was entirely free to choose her own subjects as she spent the calm
and peaceful days in pleasant conversation with friends who
happened to pass along the walk in front of the school, where
she held forth the long days through, patiently awaiting the
dismissal bell and Dean.

After Mother found out what was going on, she took Mammy to task again. Mammy never lied about anything—she
considered it a practice both un-Christian and unreliable—
and she readily admitted being "at de school wid Deanie."
Mother repeated that Dean must be allowed to go to school
on his own and the matter seemed to be settled when Mammy
said that in the future she would walk either some distance
behind Dean or on the other side of the street so, as she said
it, "Ah kin look atter de baby."

This continued until winter weather set in and one evening Mother and Mammy were sitting by the warm fire in
the living room, Mother sewing and Mammy comfortably
settled in her rocker. "Mis Maud," she declared, "Deanie
don't need me no mo." "What do you mean, Mammy?"
Mother asked. "We all need you." "He don't," Mammy re-

peated, then added, "Ah is seed boys whut will fight dem dey own size and dem as is littler—but Deanie, he ain't never backin' down no matter de size." This sudden announcement of Dean's extracurricular activities was as unexpected as it was unpleasant to Mother, and she said, "Mammy, you must put a stop to it!" Mammy stretched her shoes nearer the fire, chuckled, and said, "Deanie—he do dat ever' time. Ah garntee he is ALLUS on top!"

As soon as Dean was big enough to carry and shoot a gun, he and Father hunted quail all over the county. They had two bird dogs, excellent setters and retrievers, but barely able to keep up with Father and Dean in the field. When they returned in the late afternoons the dogs were so tired that they remained upright only long enough to eat. Then they would crawl into their kennel and sleep the night through. But they were always ready to go the next morning, one each side of the top front step, tails wagging gently and eyes cocked toward the front door.

THERE WAS A WAR

WHEN WAR BROKE OUT IN EUROPE IN 1914, BILL AND John and I would get together in our bedroom at night, spread out some maps of that continent, get the morning newspaper, and figure out the lines of battle. This was especially true during the battle of Verdun from February to September, 1916. I don't know why this particular campaign held such interest for us, but we followed it closely day after day. As it turned out, Bill and I both saw the great battlefields, though under different circumstances and at different times. He went to France in 1925 and after his return told us that he had trudged the length and breadth of the battlegrounds there, especially Verdun. He even obtained the services of a former French soldier to guide him, on the latter's own recommendation of himself as an old acquaintance of the Americans, having, as he said, served one of our colonels during the last stages of the war as a "conducteur" of a large Pierce-Arrow limousine. I don't know whether it was during or after Bill's sojourn in Paris that he let himself become adorned with a neat Van Dyke beard. He wore it home, anyway, and when we met him at the station, Mother immediately asked if he pulled his beard inside the cover at night or let it repose outside. He did away with it in a day or so, and I never saw him wear another.

When this country entered the war in 1917, Bill was nineteen, I was seventeen, and John, fifteen. We all wanted to enter military service and each understood that the other was going to do so if possible. Only with John it was impossible, though he certainly tried his best. He was then going steady with Lucille Ramsey, a charming and attractive member of an old family of the community. They later married, but at that time were only sweethearts. Lucille came to our father one morning at the hardware store and told him that John had gone to Jackson to enlist. Father called the Adjutant General of the state, who was a friend of his, to say that he and Mother felt the country didn't need fifteen-year-old boys to fight its wars. His friend agreed at once; he would make a quick check and call back. That afternoon he returned the call, saying that he had gotten John out of the hands of the military all right, but had had to place him in the custody of the sheriff to accomplish it; that John was either remarkably persuasive or the recruiters willfully blind, or both, as he had succeeded in passing himself off as an eighteen-year-old; and that he would be put on the night train to Oxford. John was pretty dejected on his return home. He told us that unless he

could contrive to grow a beard in the meantime, he doubted
if it would do him any good to try to enlist again.

With the country at war, Bill became as restless as I had
ever known him to be. He was determined to enter military
service, but hoped it could be as an officer. He realized that
this would be difficult in view of his age and the fact that he
had quit high school and had not gone on to the University.
He told us one day that he was going to New York, where he
had received assurance of employment while visiting a friend
there. He mentioned to me that once in the city he might be
able to find some means of getting into military service other
than by enlisting as a private. He went into no further details,
which indicated that he had nothing really specific in mind.
Mother and I drove him to Memphis, where he caught a train
for New York. He was not given to discussion of his personal
affairs, even with members of his family, and this held true as
we said good-by on the station platform. He embraced Mother
warmly, as he always did, shook hands with me, and said that
he would let us know how things worked out.

When he boarded the train, it was the first time that we had
been separated. We would come together again after the war
was over for several memorable and sometimes uproarious
years; then, inevitably, each would go his separate way to do
what he had the capacity to do and to refrain from doing
what he had the capacity to withstand. Up until that day in
the station at Memphis our lives, together with those of our
parents and brothers, had been as one in a closely knit and
self-sustaining family unit. Up until that day Bill and I had
shared the same bedroom, roamed the same countryside,
played the same games, eaten at the same table, and generally
read the same books. In short, the day-to-day life of one had
been the same as that of the other.

Ours was not a letter-writing family as far as the menfolks were concerned. I doubt if our father ever wrote to Bill or ever received a letter from him. I don't suppose that I received more than a dozen letters from my brother during his lifetime and these resulted from some pressing family or business matter. But we all, when away from home, kept in close touch with Mother and she with us. Some time after Bill's departure Mother received a letter from him, from, of all places, Toronto, Canada. He said that he had enlisted in the Royal Air Force Canada (as it was known in those days) and was taking flight training. This meant that, having been accepted by that country, he must have somehow convinced the authorities there that he was either Canadian or English. I do not know what guile he used, but whatever it was, it was sufficient to get him accepted as a loyal subject of the Crown.

His military service did not last very long—the war ended before he could get overseas—nor did it cover a great deal of territory, except vertically. But it did get him commissioned as a Second Leftenant (Lieutenant) and teach him how to fly. He got his pips and wings just before the Armistice, then was promptly discharged with his whole class when the end of the war came.

I did not see him again until after I came home from France the following year. I asked him what he thought about flying airplanes. "Nothing to equal it," he replied. Then I asked him if he had had a crackup or experienced any other untoward event in his flying. "Yes," he said, "I did, as a matter of fact. The war quit on us before we could do anything about it. The same day they lined up the whole class, thanked us warmly for whatever it was they figured we had done to deserve it, and announced that we would be discharged the next day, which meant that we had the afternoon to celebrate the Armistice and some airplanes to use in doing it. I took up a rotary-motored Spad with a crock of bourbon in the cockpit, gave diligent attention to both, and executed some reasonably adroit chandelles, an Immelman or two, and part of what could easily have turned out to be a nearly perfect loop." "What do you mean—part of a loop?" I asked. He chuckled and replied, "That's what it was; a hangar got in the way and I flew through the roof and ended up hanging on the rafters."

When I was past my eighteenth birthday and Mother and Father finally offered no objections to my enlisting, I joined the Marine Corps in May, 1918. We were sent to the training area at Parris Island, South Carolina. For the first time in my life I was strictly on my own, and at any time during the first several weeks I would gladly have left the war to whoever might want to take my part in it. For the first time there was no one to wonder or care whether I was tired, feeling good, bad, or just plain fed up. But, then as now, no finer group of fighting men existed, and I quickly learned that one does not become qualified for membership in it through being coddled, afraid, or lacking in willingness to do his level best no matter how distasteful the task. Each Marine did his share, whole-heartedly and, equally important, without complaint. The project of making a dependable fighting man out of a boy like me who had lived a more or less sheltered life and had been called upon to do few things he didn't really want to do, was demanding and, it seemed often, never-ending.

Bayonet practice was my brutal introduction to the realiza- tion that there are times when a man can rely only on his pride to make him stand up and face, and keep on facing, the utmost efforts of another to make him wilt and retreat in the face of an onslaught, which he could willingly avoid, except that he could not live with himself thereafter. Training op- ponents were assigned on the field, and I don't recall ever being fortunate enough to find myself facing one of my size since, hardly knowing one end of the bayonet from the other, we were at first faced with battle-tested veterans of the training unit itself. The first time, forgetting that I was no longer playing a comparatively gentle game of football with my brothers at home, I was smashed back nearly off the field before I could get my wits together. But on the way I stumbled onto the certain realization that this training was real and intended to be so in a manner leaving no doubt whatever in the minds of the unwary and weak.

Though it is doubtless more difficult for some than for others, a man learns as he must. The next day the scorching sun would again boil down on us from a cloudless, unfriendly sky, and I would find myself again with the death-dealing tools of my trade—a heavy service rifle and a bayonet—facing a man armed with a weapon just as lethal and determined to shove me into the next county. But now, almost imperceptibly, the vicious training was beginning to pay off, even for me; I quit feeling sorry for myself about the heat, homesickness, and frustration. Here, also with upraised bayonet and seemingly anxious to cut out my heart, was another recruit, not much larger than and probably just as scared as I was.

It is a good feeling for a man or boy to get control of himself when the moment of make-or-break arrives. So it was with me one day as I awaited the signal to engage my opponent. For the first time, the old, unhappy dread had been completely displaced by determination and faith, and when the sergeant bellowed "Charge," it was, I think, Recruit Falkner who was first off the line. I leaped upon my unsuspecting and unprepared opponent before either of us realized what was happening, and we went at it tooth and nail—or, rather, bayonet and rifle butt. The end came even quicker than I had expected (provided I had expected anything at all), since my overwhelming determination was not to allow myself to be shoved back again as I had been day after day. Within less time than it takes to relate it, I had shoved him back several feet and we were on the ground, but this time I was on top with my bayonet held firmly across his chest. At this moment, on the hard-baked drill field and in the presence of the hard-baked soldiers and recruits, I felt that I had become a man.

We departed a short time later for advanced, final training at the Marine Base at Quantico, Virginia, with the understanding that those making this trip had passed muster and would soon be overseas. I had now turned nineteen, and, while I might not have become a man yet, I was certainly no longer the bumbling, scared, and inept boy who had arrived at Parris Island two months before. The deadly serious and unrelenting training had taught me to stand on my own two feet, give more than I got, ask and expect no favors, and feel certain that I could serve my country, my family, and myself with honor.

The training at Quantico was even more extensive and exacting than that at Parris Island, but now we were hardened to it and took it all in stride. We had been there about a month when the next draft for overseas was made out, and my name was on it. We shipped out of New York on a captured German vessel, the S.S. *Von Steuben*, converted into a military transport, and landed at Brest in August, 1918. I had expected that we would be welcomed by the natives with wild abandon and enthusiasm, flags, marching bands, and perhaps a cookie or a flower. Instead, as we debarked the people of the city went casually about their personal affairs without so much as a glance at our beaming and would-be friendly faces. I stopped feeling hurt and snubbed when I realized that these people had been living with a war for more than four years and that one soldier was pretty much like another—he arrived, moved on to the front, and was heard of no more.

After a night in pup tents just outside the city, we were herded into the infamous "forty-and-eights" (forty men or eight horses, though, happily for each, not at the same time), the tiny, bumpy, foul-smelling French freight cars. The extreme discomfort of the "forty-and-eights" was exceeded only by the exasperatingly slow, hesitant, and clanking crawl across the lovely face of that country. Perhaps since that time someone has devised a meaner and more discouraging way to go to war, but this was surely the best (or worst) contrived in 1918.

On arrival at the replacement depot, about twenty-five kilometers behind the lines, we were quickly assigned to a combat unit, I to the 66th Company of the 5th Regiment of Marines. There were only three regiments of that famous corps in the American Expeditionary Forces in France, one on duty in Paris and the other two, the 5th and 6th, constituting one of the two brigades of the 2nd Division. They had been through the fierce fighting at Belleau Woods and Soissons, had been considerably depleted, and we joined them as replacements for the casualties which had occurred in those battles.

Little time was lost at the replacement depot. The day after our arrival we set out on foot, each man carrying a pack weighing some fifty pounds strapped across his shoulders. Our destination was the Marine brigade a short distance behind the front near Saint-Mihiel. It was raining and had been for days; mud was deep everywhere, and we slogged through it the whole night, walking fifty minutes, then dropping down into our muddy tracks for a ten-minute rest, then on again. Toward morning, for the first time, we began to hear the sounds of battle, at first only the roar of cannon, then, as we neared the front, the spasmodic clatter of machine-gun fire and the clear-cut "wham" of a rifle. Then we were no longer on a road, but were trudging single file through fields and woods. Soon we passed artillery positions and could easily see the blast of the pieces as they fired. Otherwise, the only lights anywhere were the small range-finder points of illumination among the trees here and there.

Word was passed down the line in the darkness and rain, "Close up!" We closed files, one Marine right behind another, and as we crawled up and out of a ditch we could see the war, or at least one small segment of it. Through the dripping leaves and brush we would see flashes directly in front of us and above these, some far and others near, some at full brilliance and others dying out, the star shells being shot up over the battlefield. The man in front of me stopped abruptly in his tracks; I did the same of necessity; so did the one behind me, and so on down the line. It was almost daylight, and an officer, buttoned up in a trenchcoat, came down the motionless line of men, giving orders to each sergeant he came upon. Word came down the line, passed from man to man, "Follow me." The sergeant in my section led off and we followed in line to an area of tall, gnarled trees beside a pockmarked cart trail. This turned out to be the bivouac area of the 5th Regiment, our destination.

The Marines of the various units into which we had been assimilated were, for the most part, professionals in the purest sense. Many of them were hardbitten veterans of campaigns around the world: China, the Philippines, Nicaragua and others, including, of course, Belleau Woods and Soissons in the present war, the sternest and costliest battles of them all. Their language was hardly that of the drawing room, but their acts were the heroics of which history is made. This especially applied to the longtime line and gunnery sergeants, many of whom were in their element only on the field of battle. It was their chosen way of life (or death), and I'm sure that none would have had it changed.

Later I came to know how the battle-tested veterans must have regarded us on first and unpromising sight. We were, of course, by their standards, still wet behind the ears, with no reference to the steady rain through which we had tramped all night. We were truly innocents abroad, which would be rectified in due time, but at that moment we had drunk no French wine, red or white; we had not yet shot craps between delicate mounds of manure in French barnyards; nor had we contrived to get ourselves shot at.

Shortly after midnight we took up the forward movement again, this time as members of a Marine fighting unit en route to earn our keep. We were going into action for the first time near the small village of Saint-Mihiel. We came under enemy shellfire during the morning and shortly thereafter were deployed in line of attack. I remember it as though it were yesterday. The sun had finally come out and the hilly, wooded countryside was beautiful. My first thought was that wars ought to be fought in uglier places. The division we were relieving began passing through our line on their way to the rear. They were bringing out some dead and wounded with them and were, for the most part, silent and preoccupied, though I remember one or two holding up a hand as he passed and saying, "Good luck."

Then there was nothing between us and the enemy, and our platoon lieutenant moved out a few places in front. With rifles at the ready—bayonet unsheathed, full-loaded clip in the cartridge chamber, and safety off—we came upon one of the numerous small stone hedges which abounded in the vicinity. We were on the side of a gentle slope downward, and the stone hedge made a perfect arc about the center of the slope. At the bottom the trees were much thicker than on the side.

When we were within a few paces of the hedge, machine-gun
fire opened up from the woods below. For the first time in
my life, I realized someone was trying to kill me. This applied
to every man in the regiment as well, but war is an intensely
personal matter, especially when you are being shot at. For
a fleeting second you have the inescapable feeling that you are
the only soldier on your side of the battlefield. The lieutenant,
his pistol in hand, motioned us forward and pointed to the
stone fence. As we headed toward it, I heard an abrupt but
smothered cry from the left—someone must have been hit,
but I could not see him. I saw my first dead man on a battlefield a few moments later when, after dropping down behind
the fence, I shoved my rifle over it as a sort of parapet and
there, almost directly beneath the barrel and just beyond the
base of the stones, lay the lifeless body of a German soldier.
His oversized gray uniform was as ill-fitting as my own; one
heavy, boot-clad leg was stretched stiffly out at full length,
the other pulled up at a grotesque angle as though to escape
pain or, perhaps, to try to make it more bearable; his hands
were spread outward as though in fear or supplication; and
his blond head was facing upward toward the blue sky. His age
must have been about my own.

The attack was pressed forward. There were other slopes
to go down and others to go up, open spaces to cross, and dense
woods to push through—and there was always the enemy.
Some of us were wounded and some were killed, but all did
what he had to do. What does a nineteen-year-old boy think
about when his sole task is to kill others to keep them from
killing him? For the most part he doesn't have time to think
about anything but the business at hand. Fear almost throttles
him, especially during the first few moments of an attack, any
attack. He certainly never entirely overcomes it, but he does
continue in spite of it, and I think this may be attributed to

his love of family and country, his own self-respect and, certainly, as far as the marines are concerned, his pride in that remarkable corps. He thinks of his loved ones at home, possibly with more intense affection than when he is there. Before I left home Mother gave me a small Bible with a photograph of my little brother Dean in it. It was taken when he was about five or six, and, when I would look at it while sitting in a muddy trench or on a straw mat in a barn, I would think of what a lovely child he was and how much he meant to us all. He lived barely long enough to see his twenty-eighth birthday.

After Saint-Mihiel we were next in action at Epinal, this time brigaded with a French division, which resulted in each Marine's receiving his daily quota of wine just as his French compatriots did. It also resulted in my receiving, long after the war was over, a brigade citation from the French government which Mother kept framed on the wall in the hall at her home until her death.

At Epinal we advanced over the 1914 and 1915 battlefields; relics were everywhere: smashed helmets, French and German; rotten pieces of uniforms, some hanging on tree branches and gently swaying in the breeze; crosses marking the dead; and trenches now and then to indicate the living. It was now October, 1918, and rumor had it that the next battle would be big enough to knock the enemy out of the war once and for all. Replacements began to arrive for those we had lost at Saint-Mihiel and Epinal. They were new men just over from the States, as we had been a few months before. And now we were no longer rookies, for ever since our arrival in France (how far away it seemed), danger and hardship had been our lot. Death had come to some and been seen by all; mutilation and destruction had become as commonplace as cooties and hardtack.

We had been moved up to an assembly area not far from

the Argonne Forest, and as night was falling on the thirty-first we began moving forward to take our place in the line. Again the long, silent columns, each man with his own thoughts, each with his own fears. About three o'clock in the morning we reached a comparatively open field in the woods, over which enemy star shells (or Very lights) were bursting. Our first casualties of the night occurred when some men were struck by shrapnel as we moved across the open field. Word was passed down the column that we were headed for some old trenches (from 1915) at the far end of the field, where we would seek such cover as they afforded and wait for jump-off time at daybreak.

Star shells continued to burst high overhead. These made us clearly visible, but there was nothing we could do except slog on toward the trenches. We would gladly have sprinted toward them, but the word has to be qualified when one is speaking of a soldier with a full pack on his back, an extra bandolier of cartridges slung across his shoulder, at least one pocket filled with hand grenades, and carrying a heavy rifle with a bayonet. Under such circumstances, we moved forward not by rods and miles, but rather by feet and inches.

Finally we could make out the outline of the trenches, a dark, irregular band traversing the field as far as we could see in either direction. We crawled down into them with as much speed as we could muster. We were checking our equipment as we crouched in the mud, when all of a sudden there seemed to be a thousand enemy star shells in the air at once, making the whole area almost as light as day. This was followed by the first artillery shell to explode in our immediate vicinity. It was in midair and somewhat forward and to the right of our position. Within a few seconds another swished directly over us and exploded in the mud behind our section of the trench. Fragments of the shell thumped into the ground and walls of the trench. Then our platoon sergeant called out from his position a few paces down the trench, "Down, damn it, down in the trench!"

At that instant I felt as though someone had slipped up beside me and blasted my head with a steel rail. My rifle was knocked out of my hands, and I dug handfuls of mud out of the side of the trench trying to keep from toppling over on my back in the bottom of it. It didn't work, and the next thing I knew I was flat on my back in the three years' accumulation of dank, oozy slime at the bottom of the trench. Two marines were bending over me; someone was groaning a few steps away, and I could barely hear someone calling, "Medic! Medic! This way!" The platoon sergeant came crawling up, looked at me, and asked how bad I was hit. He said, "Looks like you caught it this time. Here's your tin hat. There's a hole in it and some blood on your face. Hold tight and we'll get some medics and a stretcher up here to get you to first aid." I appreciated his kindly interest, but there certainly wasn't much chance that I wouldn't stay put. I was not exactly unconscious, but clear thoughts were hard to come by. I noticed that my right trouser leg was ripped open, and when I put my hand on it, I found blood there too. Soon the medics came with a stretcher, placed me on it, and strapped my tin hat to an arm, saying that I might want to keep it as a souvenir. Besides, the hole in it would show the doctor just where I had been hit.

By the time they lifted me out of the trench, several other wounded were on stretchers just behind it, and artillery shells were exploding all around. We started out for the first aid station a short distance to the rear. Did I pray? I don't remember. Certainly I was scared enough, or perhaps I was too scared; maybe, to the extent that I could think, I was too occupied in wondering what the doctors could do to help me before I got around to asking the Good Lord to lend a hand. After a few moments the two medics carrying me had ducked an explosion here and another there, and we became separated from the others. It wasn't long before I felt the stretcher being placed on the muddy ground again, and by the light of a star shell floating down almost directly overhead I could make out the two medics stretched flat on the ground beside me. One pulled himself along until his head was a few inches from mine and told me that we were resting in a small depression, that they had decided to get us all on the ground until the enemy barrage began to lift, and that we would then make a run for the thick woods to the rear. I could see and feel the explosions all about us and the bright star shells overhead, and I could understand their reasoning. Still, I couldn't help wondering if I were going to be hit a second time, since I had been unable to get away quickly enough the first time. While we lay glued to the ground, the second wave of the attack (we had been the first) passed by us, and I could see a man here and there abruptly stop as though he had run into a brick wall, then sway gently, or drop at once like a sack of cement to the ground.

The medics attached to the Marines in France were actually naval pharmacist mates, and the danger in which they lived was no less than that of the Marines they served with so much courage. I never saw one I would not have been proud to call brother. The cry of "medic" had hardly gone up from the second wave before the two with me jumped to their feet and ran to the wounded nearby. As soon as they had given first aid to those fallen, they came back to me, took up the stretcher again and said that they hoped I could hang on, because we were going through to the woods this time. We made it, and I was deposited at the first aid dressing station, where a doctor made a quick check and told me that my knee had been only slightly scraped by a piece of shrapnel; the head wound could not be catalogued so readily. I was given anesthesia, and the doctors probed the head wound, from which they extracted a small piece of shrapnel. My stretcher was then put in a row with those of other wounded on the wooden floor of the dressing station tent. In about an hour the doctor returned and said that he was not certain, but it appeared that the shrapnel had lodged against my skull but not penetrated it, and I was being immediately sent to a base hospital so the extent of the damage could be definitely determined.

By ambulance and hospital train I finally arrived late that night at a large United States base hospital just outside Paris and was taken almost immediately to the operating table again. When I regained consciousness several hours later, the nurse told me that I was a very lucky boy as she handed me a small piece of shell fragment which they had extracted. Thorough examination had shown this to be the last, and my skull had not been damaged. She assured me that I would fully recover before very long and I could keep the souvenir. I took it home with me and handed it to Mother just as it was given to me, on a bloodstained piece of gauze. She kept it, along with my French Brigade citation, all the days of her life. I don't know what became of it thereafter. And I suppose it doesn't matter after forty-eight years.

The war was over for me. The Armistice was signed while I was still in the Paris hospital, and with other walking patients I was allowed to go into the city so we could see the festivities. I was the only Marine in the group, and when the celebrating citizens noticed the marine emblem on my overseas cap they invariably called out, "Ah—une Marine Americaine! Un soldat, un vrai soldat!" I was indeed proud, as anyone should be who is privileged to wear this military mark of distinction. Next I was sent to a convalescent hospital at

Hyéres on the French Mediterranean, where I spent two months enjoying the sun outside and shooting craps inside. Then to the port of Saint-Nazaire and home, landing at Hampton Roads, Virginia, in March, 1919, somewhat wiser, considerably tougher, and, I thought, ready to submit myself to whatever destiny had in store for me.

Several years after the war was over I received at Oxford a small box and a big letter from Marine Headquarters. The one contained a Purple Heart (as everlasting evidence that I forgot to duck) and the other specified where my lack of presence of mind or memory, or both, had caught up with me—Argonne Forest, November 1, 1918.

After I returned home, Mother told me of a conversation she had had with Mammy following the receipt of one of my letters from France. It was in the winter and she took the letter into the living room to read it. Mammy was sitting quietly beside the fire in her rocking chair. The family had already been advised that I had been wounded in action and this was the first letter from me thereafter.

Mammy remained silent while Mother quickly read my letter, then turned to her and said, "Mis Maud—is Jackie gwine come home to us lak he is left?" Mother explained to her that I was in an army hospital, but that I had said there was nothing to worry about, for I would soon be as good as new. Mammy took the snuff stick out of her mouth, clasped her small hands in her lap, leaned forward toward the fireplace, and said, "Us thanks de good Lawd, Mis Maud, us thanks de good Lawd." She rocked gently back and forth for a few moments and turned to Mother again. "Mis Maud," she asked, "whereat is dis here France?" Mother replied that it was far away across the sea. "How far?" Mammy wanted to know. Mother told her that France was several thousand miles from the nearest port and across the wide Atlantic.

Mammy was as unable to figure out a "port" as she was an "Atlantic," but the great Mississippi River was wide—she had crossed it and knew there was a foreign land on the other side. She replenished her lower lip with another pinch of snuff and turned to Mother once again. "Mis Maud," she said, "dis here France where de Germs is shot Jackie—hit sho'ly be's jest t'other side uv Arkinsaw!"

Ah, Mammy—valiant and loyal Mammy Callie—surely never another like you.

8 AN INSPECTOR CALLS

THE FIRST WORLD WAR GOT ME A PURPLE HEART. IT ALSO escalated me out of high school. After we got into the war I found it increasingly difficult to concentrate on history, Latin, and so forth, and this resulted in a gradual disassociation from the activities of the Oxford school system. Eventually, I had so separated myself from the affairs of that institution that when I did favor the school staff with a glimpse of my bright and shining face after an absence of about two weeks, they promptly mistook me for Bill, who hadn't been around for two years. It was truly discouraging and left me with the distinct impression that my personality was in urgent need of some polishing.

Whatever the case, the good folks at the high school must have had enough of me. My return from the war may even have precipitated their announcement that all of us were heroes and that those of us who had left the school in our final year to enlist would officially be considered as having graduated. This would be attested to by proper certificates which would be mailed to us, and we would not, therefore, need to revisit our alma mater to get them. When I mentioned this unexpected, happy turn of events to Bill, he considered it a moment, smiled (after all, he had been in the war, too), and asked me whether I figured the miscellaneous facts I had picked up in France had made up for what I had more or less disdained at the Oxford school. It was a good question, and as I fell to fair reflection on the four-letter words, the crap games, and one thing or another, I realized that I could but wonder myself. In idle moments, I still do.

Bill and I entered the University of Mississippi in the fall of 1919, he as a special student and I to study law. Our grandfather Falkner, our father, and our Uncle John, while attending this institution, had become members of the Sigma Alpha Epsilon fraternity. Some time before Bill and I matriculated the governor of the state had developed an active distaste for such societies and had had them banned from the school. Some continued to operate sub-rosa, including SAE, and Bill and I, largely because of the name we bore, I suppose, were initiated into it. The membership brought us some friends, though whether one depended on the other may be open to question. At any rate, we were glad to be members of SAE and were heartily in favor of the other male Falkners' taking the same course as they came along. I believe it was just about the only club either Bill or I ever joined. But the authorities found out that the fraternities were in existence (how, we never knew), and we had to leave the school. As far as Bill was concerned this caused no undue hardship, or perhaps even inconvenience. But it was several months before the authorities relented and let us return to classes, which caused me to scurry about to make up for lost time and get my law degree in 1922.

I had barely gotten settled again when an unpredictable event, at once trifling, yet near disastrous, engulfed me and cast yet another sinister mark on my standing, such as it was, at the University: I got caught in a crap game. It filled me with shame—not the crap shooting, but, as an ex-Marine, getting caught at it. Our father was then secretary and business manager at the University and we lived in a fine, old brick residence furnished him on the campus. There was a standard punishment for shooting (getting caught at) craps on the campus—the offender was forthwith banished from residence upon it. That is to say, during the period of his faculty sentence his presence was permitted on the campus only to attend classes. This seemed reasonable enough; it prohibited the wrongdoer from contaminating the righteous except under strict faculty supervision. And it may well have offered a mild deterrent to some who lived off campus. My situation was a little different. In the first place, I lived in the bosom of my family and there was no other place to which I could repair, not short of the poorhouse anyway; and in the second place, I was loser in the game when we were caught. Thus I was among those who had paid to learn the hard way that I could throw treys (not to mention an occasional snake-eye as well as some soul-shattering box cars) with much greater frequency than I could negotiate some welcome sevens and elevens.

Another crap game I remember involved Bill. Sometime in the early twenties he and I had occasion to be in Memphis at the same time. We were staying at the Peabody Hotel and one day at noon Bill came to our room as I was preparing to leave it. He had been drinking and asked me if I had any money left. I told him that I did, about twenty dollars. He said he wanted to borrow it. I knew that he had several times that much when he left the room that morning and that he would tell me what became of it if he wanted to, otherwise not. I handed him the money I had and he started toward the door. On reaching it he stopped, turned around, and stated in a matter-of-fact tone that he had lost his money in a crap game. I asked him if he was going back to the same one, and when he confirmed that he was, I asked him if he thought the twenty would go the way of the rest. He looked at me again and said, "It probably will. But I've got to go back." Then he surprised me by asking if I wanted to come along.

I had no illusions that he was going to win his own money back, or even be able to hang onto the twenty dollars he got from me, and I certainly had no desire to see him fleeced. Still, I thought, given a little time I might be able to talk him out of throwing good money after bad. It didn't work, of course, and I should have known better than to try. As we walked in the hot noonday sun down Main Street, I pointed out the apparent hopelessness of the project, but he paid no more attention to what I was saying than he would have had I been discussing the Women's Christian Temperance Union.

We turned in at a dilapidated brownstone building on North Main and Bill knocked resolutely on the door, which was opened by a seedy looking character who, like Bill, had obviously been hitting the bottle. Without saying a word to either of us he picked up a jug of corn liquor from a table propped against the wall and tilted the spout to his lips. Though I was standing some three feet away I shuddered as the fiery liquor gurgled down his throat. Finally he took his lips away, ran his index finger through the loop in the handle, and let the jug swing gently to and fro beside his right leg. With his other hand he wiped his forehead as he looked straight ahead at the crumbling wall and said, "Aah-aah. Eeyie!"

Bill reached over, took the jug from the man's crooked finger, and passed it on to me. I took the proffered jug and raised it to my lips, wondering as I always did how a man could bring himself to partake of something so murderous to the taste and so repellant to the smell. It being my first drink of the day, I took only enough to set fire to my throat and contort my stomach. I handed the jug back to Bill and he availed himself of a sizable draught, galvanization of his throat having already set in several hours ago.

Now that the amenities of the occasion had been observed as protocol and thirst demanded, our good host had a word (or, rather, a sign) for us. Without even turning his head he raised a skinny arm and pointed a finger straight up. Bill said, "Follow me," and we climbed up two flights of rickety stairs and entered what must have been at one time a dining room or a master bedroom. There were several broken and battered cane-bottomed chairs piled up in a heap in one corner. On one wall was a cracked mirror hanging precariously by a rusty piece of baling wire hung over a bent nail protruding from the crumbling plaster of the wall.

There was no fan in the room and only one window was open, and that but a few inches. So oppressive was the heat and so silent were the players that one could almost hear the perspiration dripping from them as they stood in a circle around the only piece of solid furniture in the room, a big, round table over which was stretched a freshly laundered bed sheet, as out of place as a napkin tied about the neck of a pig. Not a word was spoken. The man I took to be next in line to throw the dice held them in the upraised palm of his

hand and stared at them intently, as though he had never
seen the likes before.

Bill took a place in the circle and pulled his (my) twenty
dollars from his pocket. I assumed that he would start out
betting at a gradual pace to see if his luck had turned, but I
had underestimated his determination to be done with the
whole affair without delay and no matter the cost. The man
with the dice dropped a ten dollar bill on the sheet and Bill
promptly covered it; then, before the man could roll the dice,
Bill announced that he had ten more dollars that said the
thrower could not pass. This second bet was covered by the
time he got his last ten dollars on the table and the man with
the dice rattled them in his cupped hand, then with a short,
curving motion rolled them and drops of sweat across the
center of the table. Bill had already backed away from the
table even before I heard someone say, "A natural eleven,
baby, a natural eleven!"

I followed Bill down the rickety stairs again and this time
he did not even stop in the dim and broiling hallway, where
our host was still holding the crock with his crooked index
finger, still staring at the dilapidated wall, and still saying,
"Aah-aah. Eeyie!"

I remember that Bill was quiet as we walked the hot street
on our way back to the hotel. He was certainly not happy at
having been relieved of his last dollar, nor did he indicate any
elation at being quit of the sordid surroundings where only
misfortune had attended him. Since we are all under, or subject to, uncontrollable compulsions of one sort or another, the
thought occurred to me that perhaps he felt that the only way
he could disassociate himself completely from something undesirable was to buy himself out just as he had bought himself in. I asked him how he came upon such a dump in the

first place and he replied that it wasn't difficult to do, which was doubtless true, though it wasn't characteristic of him to seek the likes of it. I never heard of his having anything to do with another.

Our grandfather Falkner died the year I got my degree. I do not recall his ever being sick, and so far as I know he never saw the inside of a hospital. The end came for him one quiet afternoon when, after his usual hearty midday dinner, he lay down on his bed for his daily nap, went to sleep, and never waked up again. He was seventy-four.

He was laid to rest in the family plot beside Granny, and during the funeral services Bill said something that has remained in my memory to this day. It resulted from the Colonel's trait, present in every Falkner I ever knew, of liking some people a lot and disliking others to the point of detestation. He had been a member of the Masonic Order, and the "brothers" were conducting the graveside ceremonies in accord with the rites of their organization. This included each member's slowly dumping a shovelful of earth upon the coffin as it rested on the bottom of the grave. As the men passed solemnly by, each receiving the shovel from the one who preceded him, Bill turned to me and in a low voice told me to note the third and fourth men in the line. I recognized them as two individuals for whom the Colonel had as little admiration while alive as he probably now had in his grave. I nodded and Bill said, "When the Colonel was alive he wouldn't speak to them. Now that he's dead, they throw dirt in his face."

In the meantime, Bill had contrived—I know not by what means—to get himself appointed postmaster at the small post office on the campus. It never ceased to amaze us all: here was a man so little attracted to mail that he never read his own being solemnly appointed as, one might say, the custodian of that belonging to others. It was also amazing that under his trusteeship any mail ever actually got delivered. Certain it is that none did without repeated and sustained supplications. As might be expected, sooner or later some irate clients took their desperate plight to Washington. Whether it was the first complaint of this nature we had no way of knowing; perhaps what lamentations the authorities heard went into considerably more detail than was customary. Anyway, the postal inspector who soon descended upon us (I include myself and others in the same category because our postmaster had by now appointed us as part-time clerks, two hours, three days a week payroll time for each) was armed with an inordinately large sheaf of directives, orders, and complaint forms, some of which, we noted with interest, had been filled out and signed by citizens of our quiet community.

Whether any of the complainants had actually accused us of misdirecting mail I do not know. But I do remember how deeply touched we were when the good inspector, after having pulled and pushed the loaded mail sacks about so that he could find work room, reported he had determined that all the mail addressed to our booming postal emporium was not only still there and intact but had not even been removed from the original bags.

He went to great pains to explain to us that mail is, in a sense, a public trust,—that is, until it is delivered into the receiver's hands—which had been the universal case in every office he had ever seen, except this one; and that mail is sacred and must always go through (though we would have been most happy to know, he failed to inform us "through what?"). Finally, he pointed out that we had contrived to foul up a little fourth-class office more completely than some of the best in the business had managed to do with a big first-class one, where one would assume the opportunities for fouling up would be more prevalent.

As earnest as we fully credited the inspector with being and as anxious as we were to arrive at an understanding with him, we were getting a little befuddled. The sacred business, for instance: we found it pretty difficult to see a connection between Christian precepts and a seed catalogue or a speech by our congressman sent in a franked envelope, unheard when spoken and unread when printed. As for the public trust part, we were public all right, and we trusted practically everyone—except, of course, on the golf course or at the crap table. And as for the mail getting through, we never refused a sack at the station and had to lug each one up University hill on our weak but willing shoulders, because our superiors in Washington had not seen fit to supply us with a cart, and our wheelbarrow had long since fallen apart.

While we were all dutifully wrapped up in our several labors at the post office, we were ever mindful of the idea that man does not live by work alone. For instance, there were the fine mornings when the whole vacant university golf course awaited our daily onslaughts on par, and the cheerful afternoons when, following our earnest efforts on the golf course, the restful and comforting tea hour at the post office attended to our social needs.

I remember the postal inspector as a conscientious, hardworking public servant. It did our hearts good to see such devotion to duty, and we did not even complain when, from time to time, we had to temporarily relinquish our seats at the tea or Mah Jongg table while he opened yet another virgin mail sack. After sifting through congressional circulars, mail order catalogues, and instructions on how to operate a post office, he actually came up with some of the mail about which our less patient customers had complained.

Finally the inspection was completed, but, oddly enough, the inspector stayed on for several days. One would have thought, to hear him talk, that he could hardly wait to shake the dust of Oxford from his feet. During this period he had some earnest conversations with Bill—or, rather, he talked a lot and Bill sat quietly and listened. The inspector appeared to be a man who deserved a better fate than to be confronted, as he was, with a situation so extraordinary that he could find no departmental rules (among the untold thousands with which every government agency is infested) that would cover what he had so industriously uncovered. He could not accuse us of having misdirected mail which we had never touched, or of concealing that which we had never seen. Bill wasn't postmaster much longer. I don't know exactly what happened—I had in the meantime gone to work for the Treasury Department in Washington. Perhaps the good inspector finally solved the whole thing by recommending to his superiors that Bill just wasn't the true postmaster type, even fourth class.

During the years immediately after my graduation from the University, I had not only worked part-time in the post office but had also looked after Uncle John's law office (he had been appointed to the bench). But during the long, slow summer days, at least, my brothers and I spent a great deal of our time on the golf course. As a matter of fact, we had the course pretty much to ourselves. It was like being a millionaire with a private golf course—perhaps even better: the rich and mighty would probably follow certain rules of the game, whereas we were free to make our own. Every lie was prejudged unplayable until the wayward ball found itself upon a tee or an upright and accommodating turf of grass; chargeable out of bounds meant any ball knocked two or more counties away; and no drive was counted as a stroke unless the ball rolled at least one hundred yards in the general direction of the green.

The only places on the course where there was no grass at all were the greens, each being pure dirt. The course was also a cow pasture and, while evidence of their existence was all over the place, the cows seemed especially determined to leave it on the surface of the little greens. We kept a shovel at each green in order that we could assure ourselves of at least one contour putting surface. I don't know whether the presence of the shovel activated the imagination or not, but some of our golfing fraternity whose scores were on the high side and whose consciences were on the low side hit upon the idea of dragging what we generously called a "fighting chance" trough from the ball sitting cozily upon the green to the inviting cup. This left two means by which one could fail to hole out: he could turn around and belt the ball in the opposite direction or just not hit it at all.

Just forward and to the right of the third tee there was a military cemetery which contained the bodies of Confederate and Union soldiers who had fallen in battles in the vicinity. I cannot remember ever driving over, beyond, or around it; John used to say that I spent almost as much time in it as those who never left it.

My three brothers were excellent golfers and when, from time to time, we stuck to the rules of the game, they frequently broke thirty on the little nine-hole, par thirty-eight course. I broke fifty once and talked of nothing else for weeks, stopping only when no one would listen any longer. I started out batting golf right-handed, switched over to left-

handed to improve my game, then finally to a cross-hand grip
since anything was bound to bring an improvement. Bill said
that I was surely the only man in the whole history of golf
who could, with equal certainty and precision, slice every
shot, right-, left-, or cross-handed. It must have been quite a
feat.

We still played baseball several times each week during the
summer, in what we called "The Church League," and we
played with the Methodists. Bill was the pitcher, John the
shortstop, Dean an outfielder, and I was allowed to catch
when no one else showed up for the job. My three brothers
were good at baseball, as indeed they were at all sports. John
and Dean earned their letters in baseball and football
throughout high school and college, or, rather, Dean did in
his freshman year, thereafter agreeing to concentrate on baseball when the coach convinced our father that Dean's small
size could bring serious injury to him on the football field.

Father was an avid sports fan and rarely missed seeing a
game, especially if one of his sons was in the lineup. I remember John's first varsity football game. Ole Miss had been unable to disengage itself from the hash marks on its side of the
field; it was third down, and John was sent in to take over
the quarterback chores. Some nine yards were needed to make
the down and John promptly and characteristically called a
play with himself as runner. He made a good gain and when
the men were unpiled, the officials called for a measurement
to determine if he had made the necessary yardage. Mother
and Father were on the edges of their seats by the time the
referee announced that the run had failed by about six
inches. Mother sat back in resignation, but Father heatedly
offered to equip the referee and his brethren with bifocals
before the next play was called. Having no choice, John then

punted. It wasn't a very long kick, fortunately, for he was able to get downfield in time to recover his own kick when the opposition fumbled it. Then we were all standing up, and I can hear Father now as he waved his hat (which was memorable, since he was not what one might call a hat-waving man) and called out, "That's my boy! We'll show 'em!"

By this time Father had almost totally disassociated himself from the bottle. My own feeling was that he simply decided he had had enough. Moreover, there at the University he found much to interest him: his work, friends among the faculty and employees on the campus, the students themselves, especially some who had to make sacrifices to attend college. These he would help to the extent of his capabilities. Many of the students thought a great deal of him. His work hours were not long, especially during the summer months. I can see him now as he walked slowly beneath the great elm trees on the campus, their tops golden in the rays of an evening sun. He held his gold-headed cane (which had once belonged to his father) in his right hand and kept time by tapping the ground with it as he put his left foot down.

I remember that it was about this time that Father bought something he had talked about for years—a big, red roadster. It was a Buick, with a cloth top that would almost always work except when it rained and a tremendous motor, powerful enough for a racing car—and he never drove it faster than twenty-one miles an hour. I don't know how he arrived at this precise speed (or lack of it) as the most desirable, but as soon as he was done at the office in the afternoon he would come home, get the big Buick, and he and Mother would rove the countryside, at never more nor less than a sedate twenty-one miles an hour. We wondered if it was harder on him to consistently maintain such a speed or on Mother to put up with it, hour after unchanging hour.

Shortly after the abrupt termination of Bill's affiliations with the U.S. postal system, his first literary effort saw the light of day. It was a small volume of poetry entitled *The Marble Faun*, and its publication resulted largely from the efforts of his friend Phil Stone, who had gone off to Yale to study law, then came back home to practice. Only a few hundred copies of it were printed, and I recall seeing only the copy he gave Mother. It was at this time that I became aware of his further literary work. He sent a number of manuscripts to publishers in the East, and all were returned. One day a large envelope arrived at the house for him, obviously another rejected manuscript, and as Mother handed it to him he said, "This one is back from the *Saturday Evening Post*, but the day will come when they'll be glad to buy anything I write, and these too, without changing a word."

I had no ideas about the nature of his writing and, since he apparently felt no inclination to talk to me about it, I had even less to inquire about it. After all, it was his business, not mine. Even in later years, after he had gained every honor that could come to a man of literature, we never sat down and talked about his work. When a book of his was published (the same with John later) he would send me an autographed copy, never mentioning it thereafter, much less asking me what I thought of it.

I had taken up the study of law not out of any particular preference for the subject but rather because it seemed the thing for one of our generation and of my family to do. While working in Uncle John's law office, I found it a lot less difficult to get clients than to collect fees from them. Taking the easiest way out toward becoming self-supporting, I stood some trifling civil service examination (a child of the fifth grade could have made at least 90 on it) and received an appointment to shuffle official papers in a large Treasury Department office in Washington. I entered manfully on this arduous task in 1924 and, a few months later, overheard a chance remark that a young man named Hoover had become head of some outfit in the Department of Justice and was offering positions to young men between twenty-five and thirty-five years of age who held law degrees. I made inquiry and was directed to an office in an old building on Vermont Avenue. There I was ushered into the presence of an intense and pleasant man named Harold Nathan. I applied for a job, filled out some papers he handed me, and was told that I would be advised later whether I was found acceptable.

Weeks passed and I continued to shuffle papers at the Treasury Department. Then I received a letter from Mother, saying that she hoped I had done nothing undesirable to cause the presence in Oxford of two men who were asking everyone about me and the Falkner family. Several more months passed and I received an official envelope from the Department of Justice. In it was a letter over the signature of J. Edgar Hoover advising me of an offer of appointment as a special agent and requesting me to report again to the office of Mr. Nathan for further instructions. I returned there and found twelve other men of my generation from various states. Mr. Nathan told us that many had applied and that we were the few chosen for appointment.

Each of us had recently graduated from college with a degree either in law or accounting and, though we did not know it at the time, we were among the first of a new kind of investigative personnel. Mr. Hoover himself had a law degree. He had set out to establish an investigative organization within the department, not with self-styled detectives as had staffed the bureau in the past, but with young men trained in those subjects which they would need to know to conduct investigations as he felt they should be conducted. The esteem in which he is held by all good citizens of the country amply attests to the correctness of his judgment, as does the success of the organization for which he is almost solely responsible. He is a great man, and I am proud to know him and to have been a member of his remarkable unit, the FBI.

In the 1930's the Bureau would open a comprehensive training school for new agents, serving also to retrain the older ones, at Quantico, Virginia. But in 1925, when I first became a member, there was no such section in existence. We were sent instead to the New York office of the Bureau, where we underwent two weeks of a sort of familiarization course under the special agent in charge of that office. In those far-off days the idea of a special agent carrying a gun had occurred only to a member of our class, who respectfully inquired if we were to be supplied with weapons. For his question the imaginative neophyte received a hard glance from the instructor, who replied, "No—if I turned you loose with a gun someone might grab it and crack your skull before you could duck." All this changed about nine years later when, after the Lindbergh kidnaping and other kidnaping cases, Congress saw the need and authorized us to carry arms at all times, which we frequently did and sometimes had to use.

My first office of assignment was at Nashville, Tennessee, but I moved on to Memphis, Dallas, El Paso, Atlanta, and Salt Lake City. It was winter when I arrived in Salt Lake City and was sent on an assignment to Idaho, where it was even colder. I was working on a bankruptcy case which involved the reported concealment of assets of considerable value in the form of a number of bands of sheep. I am not certain that I had ever seen more than half a dozen in my life, but I saw a lot more then. I also found their natural or enforced habitat, at least in Idaho, to be far from warm, comfortable rooms and handy eating establishments. In fact, the hundreds of sheep I counted were just about as far from the agreeable haunts of civilization as a man could get and still be in the United States. I counted these gentle beasts when it was only zero, and I counted them when it was twenty below. I counted them on wide, wind-swept plains, in the abyss of deep and frigid canyons, and amid the snow-packed rocks of high, forbidding mountains, where their sure-footed and gleeful cavortings made me certain that their mamas or papas must certainly have been mountain goats. In the end I must have counted enough of these carefree beasts to put me to sleep for a thousand years, dreaming of date palms, cotton fields, and a thermometer that never descended below eighty degrees.

I was, therefore, in a highly receptive mood when I received a letter from a former agent who had resigned and accepted a position with a national credit association which, pleased with the quality of several former agents it had employed, had openings for others: the salary would be greater than the one we were getting in the Bureau and, more important, we would be given our choice of place of employment.

I resigned from the Bureau almost three years to the day after entering it and accepted a position at Memphis. The following year, 1929, when the bottom fell out of the stock market and finances tightened up, the Memphis office was closed and I was sent to Kansas City. Curtailment of business there resulted in my being transferred to Dallas, where continuing depletion of operating funds forced us out with no place else to be sent. I returned to Oxford and wrote a letter to the Veterans' Administration reminding them of an examination I had taken in Washington in 1925, and of a subsequent offer of employment which I declined when I was accepted by the FBI. I was told that the offer still held good.

9 "I BARE HIM ON EAGLE'S WINGS . . ."

IN 1933 I WAS AGAIN FACED WITH THE POSSIBILITY OF JOINING the growing ranks of the unemployed. My duties in the Veterans' Administration had been the investigation of War Risk Insurance cases and, as an economy measure, this work was assigned to another government investigating agency, the same FBI which I had left six years earlier. I applied for reinstatement and was fortunate in being accepted again. I reported to the Washington headquarters for a retraining course on January 2, 1934, and quickly found that events in the intervening years had brought some changes—notably that henceforth we were going all out after wrongdoers and were authorized to carry arms in the discharge of our duties.

Hardly had I arrived at my first field office of assignment, Charlotte, North Carolina, when John Dillinger blasted his way out of jail at Crown Point, Indiana, and made his escape in the sheriff's own car, which was found abandoned on a street in Chicago the next day. This was a violation of the Dyer Act—transportation of a stolen car across a state line— and it gave the Bureau authority to enter the case. The Bureau was already deeply involved in the investigation of the kidnaping of George Edward Bremer at St. Paul in January of that year. A short time after Dillinger's escape agents from all over the country were called posthaste to St. Paul, where we were assigned to special squads working solely on these two cases. There followed many months of relentless work by the FBI, always interesting, sometimes uncomfortable, and not infrequently dangerous. Ultimately, the principals were all captured or killed, though several police officers lost their lives, as did three special Bureau agents.

In the meantime, Bill had married. In speaking of it, I must go back for a moment. Among the early acquaintances we made after moving to Oxford was the Oldham family, long and comfortably established in the state. Two of the children, Estelle and Victoria, were of our own age group. The others, Dorothy and Ned, came later, the latter contemporary with our little brother Dean. They lived in a big, late-nineteenth-century-style house on South Street, directly across from the residence of our Uncle John and Aunt Sue Falkner.

Estelle and Victoria (Tochie, we called her) had a common attribute of much beauty; otherwise they were quite different. Estelle was reserved, neat, and ever "the young lady," even as a child. Not so with Tochie, whose enthusiasm and energy equalled or surpassed that of any boy. Though every house on the street had a big yard, front and back, we frequently used the wide and dusty expanse of the street as a playground. Except during the ginning season, when the farmers brought their cotton to town, there was so little traffic on the street as to leave us uninterrupted for hours on end.

I remember it was there that we played our own brand of hockey matches. We used whatever sort of small rubber ball we could find, and, as a hockey stick, a small limb with a right angle cut from any tree. Then we would choose sides, boys and girls, and flail away. Nicked shins and bruised wrists were the order of the day, expected and taken in stride until one day Tochie showed up with a new and formidable weapon—her father's niblick. It was a distressing sight, especially when we reflected that she had always more than held her own with a little bent limb like the rest of us. The prospect was frightening and the result even worse than we had anticipated. We stood up against her lethal charges for only a few moments, then limped off the "field," leaving her the complete and total conqueror.

Tochie—bright, blonde, unforgettable Tochie—died when barely out of her teens. Estelle married about the time we entered World War I and went to Hawaii, then on to the Orient. I don't think Bill ever stopped thinking of her during the years she was gone, or ever had an idea of someday marrying anyone else. I had been in and out of the FBI for the first time when I learned that she had obtained a divorce and was back home again. About 1929 I was working in Memphis and met Bill at the airport one day. I asked him how his writing was coming along, and he replied, "Slowly." Then he glanced at me and added, "I'm going to marry Estelle." It was evident that his finances could stand considerable improvement, and I suggested that the marriage might best be temporarily deferred. I got what I deserved—no reply at all.

I believe Bill never doubted his ability to eventually succeed as an author. Anyway, it wasn't long after he and Estelle were married that the *Saturday Evening Post* began buying some of his stories, and he had at least one other book published during this period.

Our father died in 1932. Like his father before him, he died in his sleep—simply retired for the night and never awakened. By this time Bill was beginning to make a name for himself, but I don't recall ever hearing Father say anything about his writing, one way or another. Bill's only child, Jill, was born the following year, and I was proud when he and Estelle made me her godfather. She grew up to be a fine young woman, with her mother's beauty and charm and her father's love for animals and the outdoors.

As Bill's fortunes changed, so did his way of life. He bought a fine old slave-built home in Oxford and took up what he had wanted to do ever since 1918—fly airplanes again. Captain Vernon Omlie had a flying school at Memphis (his title came from the rank he held in the army flying service during World War I). Mrs. Omlie was also a pilot of note, rare and surprising for one of her sex in those days. So far as I know, Bill had not held the controls of a plane since conducting the Spad through the hangar roof at Toronto in 1918. Now he had to start all over again—first, learning to handle the new type of airplanes and, second, taking the necessary training to qualify for a pilot's license. It didn't take him long to acquire his license and he immediately purchased a plane, a Waco four-place, cabin biplane with a 210-horsepower Continental motor.

I was in and out of Oxford a good deal in those days and made several flights with Bill in the Waco and in some open-cockpit craft of that period. Until about 1934 there was no regular airport at Oxford, and it was necessary to make use of such fields and meadows in the vicinity as were smooth and unobstructed enough to accommodate a plane. Getting in and out of them was a little nerve-wracking at times, but it all made for good pilot training, as considerable skill was frequently needed to set down, and sometimes even more to take off. Shortly after Bill got his license, E. O. "Champ" Champion, a good and valued friend of the four of us, obtained his commercial pilot's license, and he and Bill set up a small, dirt-runway airport a few miles south of town.

In the same year our little brother Dean began taking flight training from Captain Omlie. He, too, had a natural aptitude for flying and quickly obtained his commercial pilot's license and instructor's rating. I never saw a pilot whose touch on the controls of a plane was more deft, gentle, and sure than was his. Bill let Dean have the Waco to keep at the Memphis Flying Service, where Dean went into partnership with Captain Omlie. The two gave student instruction, put on air shows, and flew passengers for hire locally and on charter cross country.

By this time Dean had married Louise Hale who, in view of what fate had in store for her, was fortunately blessed with a fine and gentle character. The success of a flying service then was largely dependent on the income received from passenger flights. Dean made many such in the Waco, which was a good plane for that sort of work. It had an enclosed cabin, would carry three passengers, was stable, and would cruise at more than one hundred and twenty miles an hour, but the motor had a tendency to "swallow" exhaust valves. This means that under extreme heat and sustained pressure from extended operation the head of a valve would suddenly and without warning break off from the stem and the pilot would find himself flying a plane with no motor to pull it.

One day Dean was flying three passengers from Kansas City to Memphis and was exactly halfway over the Mississippi River approaching the latter city at an altitude of a thousand feet when the Waco's cantankerous motor abruptly "swallowed" yet another valve. The motor had to be cut off immediately. Dean was too far from the Arkansas shore to glide back to it, and there was no place to set the plane down near shore on the Memphis side, but between him and the Tennessee side of the river there was what was known as Mud Island, overgrown with short, cushiony brush. Flags flying in the breeze at Memphis told him quickly what the ground wind direction was, an all important factor in executing the maneuver with which he was faced, which was simply to get the plane on the ground in a landing from which they could all walk away.

With his sure, delicate touch on the controls he was able to make the necessary banks to approach the little island upwind, then to kill off flying speed so that the craft was at the point of total stall at the precise second when the undercarriage mushed down into the mat of soft, yielding brush. The plane came to a halt right side up just before it reached the far side of the island. No one was hurt, nor was the plane damaged by the landing.

A new valve was ordered from the factory (by this time it was likely that Dean and Captain Omlie were the most dependable valve clients in the country). They installed it and were left with only the problem of getting the craft off the island. With willing assistance from onlookers, flight students, mechanics, and others who could be badgered into lending a hand, they labored about two weeks thinning out a path through the weeds and leveling off the ground until it appeared that a takeoff was reasonably possible. To lighten the plane they dumped out everything that wasn't essential to flight, including all gasoline except just enough to get it to the Memphis airport.

There was no question about who would fly the plane out. Dean had set it down and he would get it off again. When everything was ready he got aboard, cranked the motor and warmed it to operating temperature, then taxied to the downwind edge of the island, where he turned the plane's face into the wind with the tail wheel just at the edge of the water. He set the controls for takeoff, held tight on the brake pedals, and slowly shoved the throttle all the way forward. When the motor was wide open and the plane straining under the pull of the propeller, he released the brakes and pushed the control yoke to the dashboard. The craft lunged forward and began picking up speed at once. It would need all the motor could deliver to get airborne from such a short runway. Within fleeting moments the speeding plane approached the abrupt drop-off of the land into the river. Many pilots' normal instinct would have been to jerk back on the wheel and try to pull the plane into the air. It needed a pilot of Dean's capacity and knowledge of his craft to withstand that temptation so that he would have use of every available foot of runway to build up sufficient airspeed to break away from the ground. There could not have been more than a few feet of runway left when he pulled the control wheel to the rear just enough to set the wings at a gentle climbing angle. The undercarriage flicked the muddy river water for a second; then the plane began climbing away and Dean was airborne.

Another part of Dean's flying was putting on air shows from usable fields and small airports in the tri-state area of Mississippi, Tennessee, and Arkansas. This was done to generate interest among the spectators with the hope that some of them would later pay for short flights in the plane. Dean usually flew the Waco on these expeditions, because it was a good ship for acrobatics and for carrying passengers.

On the afternoon of November 10, 1935, I was listening to a Notre Dame football broadcast in the lobby of my hotel in Asheville, North Carolina, when I was paged for a long-distance call. It was from Sallie Murry's husband, Bob Williams, at Oxford; he told me that Dean's plane had cracked up and he was dead.

When I arrived in Oxford I went directly to Mother's home. No one was in the yard or about the door. I entered, and Auntee met me in the hallway and took my hands in silent anguish. Tragedy changes many things, others not at all. On the walls were the paintings Mother had done of her four sons, and in the corner of the living room was the old radio console over which Father, Dean, and I had listened to World Series games. Auntee went with me to Mother's room. On her dresser were the small, silver-framed photographs of us all and of the children of Bill and John. Mother was lying motionless on her bed, with the fingers of her small, delicate hands so tightly interlaced across her chest that they were as white as the bed sheets. I leaned over and kissed her forehead. She opened her eyes, looked at me for a moment, and said one word, "Jackie." She had to almost wrench her hands apart, so tightly were they clasped. And I thought of how cold and little was the one that brushed my cheek. How feeble was the gesture and how terribly profound was the grief behind it!

Later Bill, John, and I went into the living room and they told me what had happened. On the late afternoon of the ninth Dean had flown the Waco to an open pasture near Pontotoc, Mississippi, to spread word about the air show he would put on the following day and about the chance for local citizens to ride in a plane afterward at reasonable prices.

The next morning a number of people came out to the pasture, and Dean took off alone and performed some acrobatics in the Waco, then returned and began taking up passengers.

There resided in the community a young man who had been coming to Memphis at intervals to take flight lessons from Dean. He was big and strong, outweighing Dean by sixty pounds or more. Shortly after noon on this date the boy and two of his friends appeared at the pasture, and all three boarded the Waco, the student flyer getting in the front seat next to Dean. Takeoff was normal and the plane disappeared in a slow climb to the southwest. The usual passenger ride lasted about fifteen or twenty minutes. Thirty minutes passed and there was still no sign of the plane; then word came from a farmer some twenty miles to the southwest that a plane had spun down into his back pasture and disintegrated.

It was the Waco, ripped into a thousand pieces, the four occupants so torn and mangled that it was impossible to tell which piece of sheared flesh and bone belonged to whom. It was hard enough for Bill and John to tell Mother that her youngest son was dead; it would have been brutal beyond reason to allow her to see the pitiful heap that remained of him. Quick arrangements were made by them, and Dean was taken immediately in a closed coffin to the cemetery, where he was lowered to eternal rest not far from the grave of our father. Bill later chose the inscription for Dean's tombstone—"I bare him on eagle's wings and brought him home to me."

The Civil Aeronautics authorities made an investigation of the crash. I never saw the report, but Bill told me they had determined that when the ship crashed, the control wheel was on the side occupied by the student flyer. On that type of plane the control wheel was of the yoke, throw-over design, which meant that to put it in the hands of the person riding in the right front seat it was necessary to pull back strongly on the knob of a locking pin at the top of the vertical support column, then lift the horizontal arm with wheel attached and pull it over to the right side.

Bill, John, and I were convinced that, no matter how the student got the control wheel in his own hands, his lack of experience caused him to stall inadvertently in flight at low altitude, resulting in an immediate slip into an uncontrollable spin. Dean must have sensed at once what was happening and grasped the wheel to get the craft out of the spin before time ran out. This could be done only by immediate neutralization of the rudders and shoving the control wheel forward.

In a spin an aircraft gyrates earthward about its own axis, presenting an awesome dilemma to one who has not practiced recovery from it time after time. The inexperienced pilot sees the earth rushing toward him, and his natural impulse is to do the thing which in normal flight will get him away from the earth—pull back on the elevator control wheel. But in a spin this maneuver has the opposite effect. It tightens the rotation circle and speeds the descent. This meant that Dean had but a few seconds to disengage the wheel from the hands of the student and shove it well forward. To accomplish this he had to pull back on the yoke pin, thus tightening the vicious spin even more, while he tried to free the wheel and get it forward in the lap of the student (bigger and stronger than himself), or swing the arm over on his side and push forward on the wheel at the same time. There was neither sufficient time nor altitude left for him to accomplish either.

I doubt if anything ever happened to Bill that hurt him as much as Dean's death, and I think this is especially true because, in a real sense, he held himself responsible. He had financed Dean's flight instructions and his partnership in the flight school with Captain Omlie, and had given him free, unrestricted use of the Waco. John and I tried to make Bill realize that what he had done for Dean was what he wanted above all else; his love for airplanes was so great that, given a choice, he would have preferred to end his days on earth just as he did.

Dean's only child, named Dean after him, was born the following March. Had her father lived, he could not possibly have shown her more affection or done more for her than Bill did all the days of his life. Bill's only child Jill was a few years older than Dean, and to see the two of them with him one would have been hard put to differentiate the daughter from the niece.

It was Auntee, perhaps almost as much as Bill, who sustained Mother when Dean was killed. She and Mother had been close and affectionate friends in girlhood. When the rest of us had gone our separate ways and Mother lived alone in her home in Oxford, Auntee always found the means, no matter the inconvenience to herself, to call on her frequently.

After our father's death Mother and Auntee roved the countryside in Mother's little Chevrolet coupe. I suspect that Auntee was always the restless moving spirit behind these innocent forays. She could not drive a car, and, since many of the roads over which they rambled were unpaved and far from service stations, Auntee decided that they must have a male present in the car against the possibility of motor or tire trouble. Auntee assigned this job to a small Negro boy, who thereafter accompanied them. The little coupe had no rear seat, but it did have a rather spacious trunk compartment which became the repository for the little boy. During these drives there must have been some satisfying periods when neither the motor nor the tires required any immediate at-

tention; during these intervals all the boy had to do was enjoy
the passing scenery. But he had seen it all many times and
it is likely that his job ended up being the sort that most folks
seek all the days of their lives—all he had to do was sleep, to
such extent as the constantly swirling dust permitted.

Auntee had the biggest 38 revolver in the whole state, and
prior to setting out on a journey, she would put it carefully
in the glove compartment of the coupe, together with a hand-
ful of ammunition. She always insisted that Mother advise
her beforehand when a stop was to be made—at a small country store, a filling station, or whatnot. Then Auntee would
carefully note the surroundings, decide the extent of possible danger existing or likely to exist on the premises, and
load her revolver accordingly. I asked Mother how Auntee
arrived at the conclusion that one place merited only one or
two cartridges whereas another might deserve a full chamber. She replied that she didn't know, but that Auntee never
seemed more contented than when preparing for a possible
onslaught. Of course, the two of them were as safe touring
the countryside in the little coupe as they would have been
had they not gone abroad; still, I suspect that Auntee always
secretly hoped that somewhere, somehow they would suddenly find themselves confronted by a battalion, that all
would turn out to be Yankees and that she would instantly
annihilate the whole outfit, needing only however many cartridges she had elected to load into her revolver on that particular occasion. And had such a heart-warming event taken
place, it could be reasonably assumed that the little boy in
the trunk compartment would have slept through it all.

My three brothers and I had a common and everlasting
love for airplanes, and our mother was surely unique, or very
close to it, in having four sons who were all pilots. Neither

John nor I got our pilot's licenses until after Dean was killed. John was a civil engineer by profession, but after several years he decided that the future was not bright enough for him to remain in engineering. Shortly after Dean's death he went to Memphis and established a flying service, but alone, since Captain Omlie had been killed in a plane crash the previous year. In addition to giving flight instructions and doing charter work, he managed to get possession of an old Stinson tri-motor, seven-passenger plane which he flew on his own airline between Memphis and Helena, Arkansas, and other nearby points. He had a full captain's uniform—wings, stripes, and all. He was handsome in anything and strikingly so in that uniform.

I was the last of us to take up flying, but, though the desire had been present for years, it was not until after I got a raise in 1934 that I was in a position to do anything about it. I was in Greensboro, North Carolina, when the notification of my salary increase came through. The next day I began flight training in an open-cockpit Fairchild.

It is generally accepted, or was then, that the best way to learn to fly is to take lessons regularly from one instructor, in one aircraft, at one airport; but the nature of my work dictated that I could follow none of this advice—I had to take my instructions wherever I happened to be, under whatever instructor was available, and in whatever type of plane he happened to have at the moment. In one sense it was not bad, for this gave me a diversity of training unavailable to one who sticks to one plane, instructor, and airport.

By November, 1934, I had acquired about six hours of instruction at Greensboro and had found flying to be more appealing than anything I had ever done. At this time the instructor indicated that he would turn me loose to solo during my next lesson. But this was not to be—not in Greensboro, anyway. Before I could get back to the airport my work took me to Louisville, Kentucky, for a temporary period. When it continued to stretch out, I found time to go out to the Louisville airport one Saturday afternoon shortly before Christmas. I showed my student's permit and log book to a flight instructor there, and he took me up in a Taylor Cub. After about an hour of instruction he asked me if I could return the next week. I did, and after we had "shot" a few landings in the Cub and I had taxied the plane back to the end of the runway, the instructor tapped me on the shoulder, unbuckled his seat belt, and prepared to climb out as he spoke the magic words, "She's all yours. Take her away."

Here I was at long last, alone in an airplane and ready to take off with no one but myself to depend on. I was delighted and had no apprehensions whatever, feeling certain that I could not fail at something which had grown to mean so much to me. I lined up the craft on the runway into the wind, simultaneously pushed the stick full forward and the throttle wide open, and we began to roll down the concrete. As we picked up speed I felt the tail wheel lift from the surface, then began easing back on the stick until buoyancy of the craft could be felt, then continued pressure on the stick until the wheels lifted from the runway and we were in the air.

I climbed to the prescribed thousand feet of altitude and glanced about me with a marked feeling of exhilaration that no other experience in my life ever equalled. It was wonderful, and I even marvelled at the beauty of the aircraft, though, as a matter of fact, a homelier one than the little Cub of that period was never let out of a hangar. But to me, on my solo flight, it was the most beautiful thing ever set to wings.

A prerequisite for taking the government flight test to ob-

tain a pilot's license was fifty hours of solo flight time. Since I
had to do my flying when and where I could find time and
finances to do it, by the time I approached the required fifty
hours I had flown Aeroncas in Miami, Wacos and Birds in
Memphis, Kinners, Birds, and Stearmans in El Paso, and,
finally, Fairchilds in Albuquerque. I was taking training in
acrobatics and perfecting myself in the flight test maneuvers
at El Paso and Albuquerque in the summer of 1936 when the
instructor at the latter place told me that the Civil Aeronautics Authority inspector would be at the local field the
first week in September, and he was sure I could pass the flight
test without difficulty. I made a quick check of my flight log
book and found that I was shy about six of the required fifty
hours. I had a week before the inspector was due and was
able to get away from my work for only two more hours of
flying. Somehow or other, though—my conscience still does
not trouble me at all—when I presented myself to the inspector the following week, my log book showed a neat fifty hours
and twenty minutes of solo time. I took the test for my license
in the Fairchild, passed it and the subsequent written test
without a great deal of difficulty, and received my private
pilot's license. In a long lifetime I have received many papers,
but none ever gave me the feeling of personal pride and satisfaction that this one did.

10 A YELLOW AND BLACK AERONCA

DURING THE NEXT SEVERAL YEARS I KEPT MY PILOT'S license current by flying rented planes wherever and whenever circumstances would permit, always putting aside some savings here and there with the hope of buying a plane of my own some happy day. I had a good idea of the sort of aircraft I wanted. I read the aviation trade journals each month and, finally, in the early part of 1939, there was a "for sale" notice on the sort of plane I had in mind. It had a two-place cabin, a radial 85-horsepower motor, and air brake (or flap), cruised at 117 miles an hour, and had less than fifty-five hours on both airframe and engine. The asking price was so low that I thought there must be a misprint.

The plane was an Aeronca Low Wing; about seventy-five had been manufactured in 1936, then it was discontinued. I had never seen one but had heard the model discussed, not always favorably. It had a reputation of being able to get from one place to another at a commendable speed, provided the man flying it kept a close and attentive watch (like a preacher hovering over an unreconstructed sinner who might revert to his natural inclinations at any time). Also, it was reported to have a marked tendency to ground loop if the terrain was a little uneven or if there was a crosswind; thus the pilot's troubles were not entirely over even after he had made a landing. Even so, it had wings, and I was certain that, since it had wings, I could fly it. I got off a wire to the aircraft dealer at the Wayne County, Michigan, airport who had advertised the plane, requesting confirmation of the quoted price and low airtime, and asking whether there was a thirteen in the craft's identification number. Dean had been killed in one having two thirteens in its number. I was in Seattle at the time and received a quick reply to my wire; there was no thirteen in the identification number—it was NC 16278 (after all these years I can still rattle it off from memory); the plane and engine times were correctly quoted, as was the price. I made a quick check of my finances and was gratified to find that I could just manage it. True enough, I would likely have to cut down to one meal a day and sleep in some accommodating rescue shelter—but I would have an airplane. I sent the agent a check as binder to hold the plane for me and advised that I would be along within a short time to take delivery on it.

While I was awaiting my next salary check to finance the trip to Detroit to get the plane, I received a transfer to San Francisco, where I was kept so busy for several weeks that May had come before I could get a week's leave. My plans were to take delivery on the plane, fly home to Oxford for several days, then take the southern route on to San Francisco. I wired the agent what date I would arrive at his field and requested that he have the plane ready for flight.

I shall never forget my first sight of my airplane, and I can close my eyes at any time and see it again, as though the first time were only yesterday. It was sitting off to itself near the hangar entrance, bright yellow with black trim, paint gleaming in the shafts of a late afternoon sun. Pride of ownership welled within me as I approached it, and I thought of how fortunate I was to have at last obtained a thing I had wanted so much for so long.

Bright and early the next morning I took off in my beautiful Aeronca. There I was in my own plane setting out alone on a flight that would take me more than half way across the continent. How terribly long ago it seems as I write of it now. World War II had not yet started; Churchill was just an Englishman whose repeated warnings to his fellow citizens yet went largely unheeded; Norway, Belgium, and Holland either trusted Hitler or suspected no reason to mistrust him; colonialism was not a dirty word; civil rights were unheard of in the land; and a man was considered unworthy of notice if he was so lacking in self-respect as to expect others to do for him that which he was unable or unwilling to do for himself.

Flight conditions could not have been better than they were on that May morning in 1939; there was no turbulence in the air and visibility was practically unlimited. While my ship did not have such refinements as a radio and landing lights, it was equipped with navigation lights which operated through a small storage battery. The salesman had told me that the battery was dead, seemed to be beyond any hope of repair, and the company had no replacement for it.

I arrived at Indianapolis close to my estimated time, got the plane refueled, and fell to talking shop with some local pilots. Then I shopped about for a battery that would fit my plane in order that I could at least have navigation lights in the event of any future flying after dark. By the time my unsuccessful search was over it was too late for me to have any hope of reaching Nashville (my next stop) until well after nightfall, so I stayed in Indianapolis for the night.

I was back at the field early the following morning, and the weather reports, though passable, were not good. They showed scattered rain squalls and considerably lowered visibility all the way to Nashville, but farther to the west the weather would begin to clear during the forenoon with some strong northwesterly winds. I changed my flight plan to Memphis instead of Nashville and took off. The weatherman had judged correctly, as there were almost constant rain squalls from ground level up to four thousand feet. Above that altitude I could not go and still be able to see and check off the terrain features along my flight path. As it turned out, I was missing them in the intermittent rains from my altitude of only three thousand feet. After more than three hours in the air I realized nothing that was passing beneath me remotely fitted what should be there according to the sectional chart on the seat beside me. There was nothing to it except that I was lost.

This was far from being the first time that I had got myself lost on a cross-country flight, and I was not even particularly disturbed, for the sun was beginning to break through to the west and in that direction lay something that, short of going blind, I could not miss—the Mississippi River. Not knowing exactly where I was, I could not estimate how far I might be from the river. I set a compass course due west and was soon flying in the bright sunshine of a lovely spring day. After about forty minutes the fuel gauge told me that wherever the river happened to lie, it was beyond my capacity to reach it. The time had come when I would have to set down whether or not, and I had better use what fuel was left in making use of the most desirable place in which to do it.

It was Sunday, and I passed low over a pleasant farm house, just to the rear of which a number of people were sitting at what I took to be a sort of picnic table. Immediately beside the house was a long, apparently level, strip of short grass meadow. In those distant, happy days folks who flew planes made use of nature's and man's handiwork in manners doubt-less unthought of by today's jet pilots. As I circled over the farm house I decided that I would land on the meadow strip and then respectfully inquire of the good people at the table nearby where in tarnation I might be. Since, whenever pos-sible, a plane is landed into the wind, it is important to know the direction of it even when landing on a regular concrete runway. This information is doubly important when a pilot is preparing to land in a pasture, which is usually surrounded by trees and other obstructions, and whose ter-rain may or may not be laced with furrows or other landing gear-cracking indentations. From past experience I looked for the family clothesline and was happy to see that the lady of the house had not brought in all of her Saturday washing—several sheets and a shirt or two were blowing briskly from west to east. Then, as I circled low on the far side of the strip I saw four cows, all standing contentedly facing the east, which con-firmed what the clothes had already told me: that the pre-vailing wind was out of the west.

It would have been too much undeserved good fortune, I suppose, for the strip I had selected to run due east and west. It was nearer northwest and southeast. I banked into an ap-proach over the tall trees at the east side of the meadow, and the good folks at the table must have to a man dropped their drumsticks and well-prepared ears of early corn as each leaned toward the trim yellow and black aircraft coming in for a visit. As I came in over the elm trees I set the flaps at a full ninety degrees, pulled up the nose and applied left aileron and right rudder, then slipped forward and down to the strip. I righted the craft just above the ground and touched down in a three-point landing. The ground was so smooth that there was not even a bounce. I braked to a stop, turned about, and taxied back toward the house, where everyone was then standing beside the strip waiting for me.

Even in 1939 it wasn't every day that an industrious farmer dining quietly with his family had an unknown (or uninvited, for that matter) visitor drop in literally out of the clouds, using his meadow as a landing field, his cows as wind direction indicators, and making his hound dogs run for cover. Even so, no visitor could have been received with more courtesy and, perhaps it should be added in fairness, with more astonishment than I was. While they were inspecting my Aeronca, I was informed that I was in Tennessee, some twenty miles east of Jackson. This pleased me greatly, as it meant that I was now almost in my own backyard, although had I known how close I was to that city I needn't have run the risk of landing in the meadow.

I was less than a hundred miles from Memphis, into which my brothers and I had flown so often as to be able to get to it without half trying from any reasonable distance in any direction, provided there was sufficient fuel in the tanks. After partaking of a dish of homemade ice cream provided me at the picnic table, I thanked the family kindly for the use of the meadow, the accommodating clothes on the line, and the calm cows, and prepared to take off. It appeared unnecessary to

mention the hounds; all had cheerfully emerged from under
the barn and were then sniffing my Aeronca. To make rela-
tions even better, and surely more memorable for him, I had
the farmer get into the cabin and instructed him about what
switches to turn, pedals to push, and lever to press while I
spun the propeller to crank the motor. It caught at once as
always, exploded into a clatter that pleased and excited the
family, but again scared the daylights out of the hounds, who
tucked their tails between their legs and made another wild
dash for the underside of the barn.

I glanced at the cows and saw that they were still standing
motionless, headed downwind, not at all concerned with me
or the plane. Having set planes down in pastures almost as
often as on airport runways, I have always mildly wondered
why an airplane will first attract, then repel and almost always
scare the socks off dogs, horses, and chickens, yet have little
appreciable effect on mules and none at all on cows. Maybe it
is because dogs, horses, and chickens come equipped with a
notion that strange apparitions will nip them; while mules,
in a sense, dare them to try it, and cows just don't give a hoot
one way or the other.

I taxied quickly to the southeast corner of the meadow. The
wind was still brisk, and I was just airborne as I reached a
point opposite the farm house where the whole family stood,
waving me on my way. I took my hand off the throttle long
enough to wave back, then held the craft a few feet above the
ground to build up flying speed sufficient to clear the trees
at the end of the strip. As we approached them I heaved back
on the stick and cleared them with room to spare. It was
child's play to get to the Jackson airport, as I could easily
make out the city immediately forward a few moments after
taking off. I refilled the tanks and got a weather report—clear

and calm to the south. I called the family home and was told that Mother and Bill were in Memphis for the day, but could be reached by telephone and would be told that I would arrive at the Memphis airport within the hour. Familiar landmarks began showing up shortly after I took off for Memphis. This time it was not even necessary to have a map on the seat beside me, for this countryside and everything upon it had been etched upon my memory since childhood.

Soon the Memphis skyline came into view, together with the "S"-shaped Mississippi River and the bridge across it. There were a lot of people in 1939 who were not interested in airplanes or in those who flew them, so among the few human beings present at the airport it did not take long to distinguish Mother and Bill standing beside Mother's Chevrolet coupe next to the airport office. They knew what sort of plane I had bought and recognized my Aeronca on sight as I banked over the edge of the field at a thousand feet. They looked up and waved, and I waved back by rocking the aileron control to dip the wings in salute.

Many years have passed since that enchanted day and neither of those dear people is now living, but my memory of it will remain. How small they looked from a thousand feet as they stood side by side looking up through the golden cast of a setting sun toward a blue and cloudless sky to welcome me—not just because I had come a great distance to see and be with them, but because our family ties were so close, one member bound to the other by ties of affection and love so deep and constant that a reunion between any of us was a cherished and memorable event. How empty life must be to him who has no one to love, and how catastrophic it would be to go through life without affection from someone.

Although Mother never spoke to me about it at any time,

I'm sure she was never able to reconcile herself completely to our flying, especially after Dean's death. Perhaps her reticence resulted from her determination not to interfere with our doing something we loved so much, though I doubt not that she prayed we would give it up.

I spent two days at home and they were indeed Falkner days at the airport (named the Dean Falkner Memorial Airport). Since my plane could carry only one passenger, I spent a good portion of the time taking up almost every member of the clan, as well as some family friends. Mother was one of the first to go for a short flight over town; then there was Auntee, Bill, Sallie Murry, Cousin Katherine Sue Price, my nephews Jimmy and Chooky, Mammie Callie, Dean's widow Louise, and little Dean, then three. I was proud to take Louise for a ride, knowing how easy it would have been for her simply to say she wanted nothing to do with planes.

Auntee was enchanted by her flight with me, though it was not the first time she had been up. I think that one time or another she had flown with each of us. Flying interested her and, as always, her curiosity was practically unlimited. She glanced at the altimeter like a lively little girl looking at an unusually fascinating toy and said, "Is that right, Jack, two thousand feet up and the hand is still moving?" I assured her that she was correct and that the moving hand meant we were still climbing steadily. Seeing that it pleased her, I continued a straightaway climb until we had reached four thousand feet, then set the controls for level flight, and the airspeed indicator crept up to one hundred and twenty miles an hour. I called her attention to it, and she leaned forward to get a closer view of the instrument. As she watched I eased the nose of the ship down, and the speed quickly built up to more than one hundred and forty miles an hour. She was delighted and continued to be as I put the plane through some steep and

shallow banks and a gentle power-off stall. She enjoyed every
minute of it, and I'm sure that with a little instruction she
could have done as well on her own.

Bill flew with me for a few moments because he happened
to be at home and I wanted him to ride with me. John was
not at home; he was busy flying his own craft at his flying
service in Memphis. Mammy Callie also flew with me; she
was then in her nineties. She was so small that it took the
combined efforts of most of us to get the seat belt shortened
so that it would not wrap around her a dozen times. One had
only to know her to understand that she considered her life a
full one, and one had only to hear her talk about "dem flyin'
contraptions" to realize she did not figure that going up in
one was necessarily going to make her life any fuller or more
enjoyable. Even so, she was a member of the family, and I
would not have slighted her for any reason. When her turn
came, I held the plane door open and called, "Mammy, are
you ready for a ride with me?" She hesitated only long enough
for Mother to pat her on the shoulder; then she came resolutely to the plane.

Auntee and Bill helped her up onto the wing and then
down into the passenger seat. After Bill and I had got her
secured by the shortened belt, I closed the cabin door and
taxied the plane slowly down to the end of the runway. I
looked at Mammy; her snuff stick was as rigid in her tightly
clenched teeth as her little body was in the seat. I hesitated,
because I did not want to frighten her, and I said, "Mammy,
had you rather go back to the hangar and wait with Mother
while I take someone else up with me?" She leaned her head
over toward the cabin window, glanced at the good, solid
ground, then quickly looked up at the sky and said firmly
and without a quiver, "De fambly is went up wid you, Jackie."
"That's right, Mammy," I replied, "most of them, anyway,

but it will be all right if you just decide to stay on the ground
—no one will hold it against you." She settled back in her
seat, looked straight ahead over the cowling and said, "Whereat de fambly goes—Ah goes, too!"

And we went up, Mammy and I, through the clean, smooth
air, up in an almost effortless climb toward a blue and beckon-
ing sky that seemed to rest as a protective dome upon all crea-
tion, while low and off to the left, deeply off to the west, came
the slanting, golden rays of the setting sun that spread a benevolent canopy across the good land that had nurtured us. At
three thousand feet we leveled off at cruising speed, the sound
of the motor eased into a muted melody, and I looked at
Mammy again. The magic benediction of flight had descended
upon her, tenseness had given way to relaxation and apprehension to curiosity; she was now chewing happily on her
snuff stick and trying to lift herself high enough to look out
of the window. When she glanced at me, I smiled, and she
smiled back immediately and tapped my knee as she said, "Dis
here is good, Jackie. Dis here is GOOD!" And indeed it was.

The last day I was at home in that summer of 1939 Mother
and I talked, as we frequently did, about the family. Dean
had been dead for almost four years and I remember that we
talked of him. Little Dean had been born after Louise came
to live with Mother. Mammy, who would die the following
year, was then living in her cabin in Bill's backyard. She came
to Mother's nearly every day to "look atter de baby."

This would be the last time I was to see Mammy. The trees
were green, flowers were in full bloom, and the strong heat
of summer had not yet arrived. It was agreeably warm and
pleasant in the early afternoon, and Mother, Mammy, and I
sat on the front porch, Mammy in her rocking chair with the
newest Falkner in her arms. I looked at her and memory

carried me back more than thirty years. The town clock in the courthouse belfry a few blocks away clanged the passing hours; the small-town traffic moved leisurely along the quiet street; acquaintances of more than a third of a century passed unhurriedly along the sidewalk and smiled in greeting; and I had the feeling that even for Mammy thirty years had been somehow chopped from time and she was sitting on the front porch of a house on South Street with a baby named Dean in her arms.

There were other visitors before the long and lovely afternoon was done, among them the new generation of the family. Youth was with them as it had been with us so many years before, a shining attribute of life itself. Auntee and Sallie Murry came with the latter's charming daughters Holland and Zandra; Bill, an old slouch hat in one hand and the other leading his blonde girl child Jill; and John with his fine sons Jimmy and Chooky. It was a family get-together against my departure on the morrow.

That night I spread out my Geodetic Survey airways maps on the living room table, got out my dividers and computer, and set to work charting out the compass headings and checkpoints for the remainder of the flight to San Francisco. I knew Mother was in the room, but I was too occupied to notice what she was doing. It was not until I returned home the following year that I found out about it. She had sketched the contents of the table as I toiled over the charts. From them she did an oil painting which, with others done by her talented hand, now hangs in my home. In the painting are the charts, filed as to course, compass headings, and bearings, properly boxed by sections, the bent-over reading lamp under which I had worked, the divider, computer and, surely the most distinctive of all, my personal trademark, a half-full

sack of Bull Durham, flakes of it spilled out on the table, a
book of cigarette papers, and even several half-burned
matches.

Our Grandmother Butler had much artistic talent and a
great deal of her talent passed on to Mother, Bill, John, and
Dean. Only I was barely able to draw a straight line, and that
under considerable pressure and compelling necessity. Mother
gave little attention to painting until after the four of us
were grown and no longer underfoot. She set up an easel near
the big windows in the dining room and spent much of the
time at it during her remaining years. At first she sold her oil
paintings only in the area near home, but word about her
work passed from one group to another and eventually there
was a ready demand for her paintings throughout the country.

Mother, who knew how much breakfast meant to us all and
who was fond of that agreeable meal, liked nothing better
than to prepare it for whoever happened to be at home. I
got up early on the morning of my departure for San Francisco, and while I was busy on the telephone getting a report
from the weather bureau at the Memphis airport, she set
about to get breakfast for us. Bill came by in time to have
coffee with us, and then he and Mother took me to the airport.

Bill and I pushed my Aeronca out onto the ramp, and after
making sure that all was in order, I folded my map on the
seat for the first leg of the flight, then said good-bye to Mother
and Bill. I never saw her shed a tear at the departure of any
of us, however close she may have been to it.

I got aboard, shut and bolted the cabin door, and fastened
my belt. Bill walked around to the front of the plane to swing
the propeller. The motor caught at once, and Bill went back
over to stand beside Mother while I warmed it up. Knowing

that she was probably unconsciously comparing the Aeronca with the Waco that had taken Dean's life, I taxied on down to the end of the runway and hurried the takeoff procedure. I turned into the wind, opened the throttle, and moved down the runway with increasing speed. I caught a glimpse of Mother and Bill standing side by side and waving. I waved back at them, then quickly set about the business of getting airborne and clearing the trees on the hill below the south boundary of the field.

11 A COW AND A COUPE IN ALASKA

ON RARE, HAPPY, AND EXHILARATING OCCASIONS MAN FINDS the capacity within himself to turn bad into good or weakness into strength and, perhaps because these occasions are so rare, they lift his soul and remain imprinted in his memory forever. Such an event was my blessed lot at El Paso on my flight to the West Coast.

By the time I passed over the Arkansas-Texas line, the ceiling had lowered and the air had become turbulent, tossing and pitching the Aeronca all over the leaden sky. And when Dallas finally came into view the horizon seemed to be sweeping up and down and shifting laterally as much as the aircraft. The green light (signal for landing clearance) was beamed at me from the airport tower as soon as I was close enough to make out the field. Even though I made the final approach under power for better control, I was well down the runway before I could get both wheels on the ground at the same time. The landing roll was very short, the wind saw to that and also nearly blew the plane off the taxi strip as I inched through the driving rain to a hangar ramp.

I descended from the plane and found that my arms were as tired and my knee joints as sore as if I had ridden a bicycle from Oxford. I had only two days of leave left; it was only a little past midday, and I felt that I had to keep going. So I hurried over to the weather bureau office, only to find that a cold front was moving from the southwest across the plains toward Abilene and that within an estimated two hours the ceiling would be zero. While I was grumbling about that, the weatherman remarked, certainly with reason, that I was lucky to have gotten down in one piece at Dallas.

All this meant that there was nothing to do but stay until the weather cleared. I went to a downtown hotel, left an early call, and when it came the next morning I looked out the window at a steady drizzle and a dark, inhospitable sky. But a call to the weather bureau brought some hope—the cold front had become stationary over the Panhandle, local rains would diminish, and it was expected that visibility would increase so that takeoff to the west could be cleared by noon. Back to the airport I went, made a thorough check of my plane, and fretted away the hours. By eleven-thirty the rain had become a mild drizzle and breaks in the clouds could be seen in the west. Thirty minutes later I had clearance to take off. The green light was aimed right at me and followed me as I turned onto the runway, into a strong west wind, and took off.

Within a few moments the plane was at the prescribed

twenty-five hundred feet altitude, or as near to it as I could manage. A gust of wind would snap under a wing, the nose of the plane would swerve up, then the whole machine would drop off into a temporary vacuum, and I could feel the rudder pedals straining against my feet. So strong was the wind that it took almost twice the estimated flight time to reach the first visual checkpoint, which meant I would have to refuel long before I could begin to get altitude to clear the mountains east of El Paso.

The cold front may well have become stationary in the Panhandle, but the vile weather beating at the Aeronca and me was anything but motionless. As it turned out I was fortunate to make the Midland airport, where I could land straight in, as I probably didn't have enough gas left to circle the field. Here, I had the gasoline tanks filled to capacity and got another weather report—clear all the way to El Paso with strong winds through Guadaloupe Pass. It was now late in the afternoon, but I figured there would be enough daylight left for me to clear the mountain pass. Then I could pick up considerable airspeed with a gentle descent of less than seventy-five miles to the well-lighted El Paso airport.

But first, there was Guadaloupe Pass to contend with. With the controls set for constant climb and the craft being buffeted more than ever by the howling wind whipping down from the mountains, I approached the mountains at what seemed to be a snail's pace. By the time I had crept up to an indicated seventy-five hundred feet, I could see the dim and distant horizon, which meant that I was above the highest point in the pass. And now the flight had become as rough as any I had ever known, and it was sure to become worse when I actually crossed the mountains. I could only hope that the muscles in my legs and arms would not lock and that the fabric on the plane would not disintegrate.

Disenchantment is not easily borne, especially when it concerns something heretofore loved in totality. It begins with nagging doubts that hurt, mystify, and repel: and I was hurt, mystified, and repelled as I worked the Aeronca through the pass in a high, lonely, darkening, and windswept world. Finally, we cleared the pass, and there was just enough daylight left for me to locate the single highway leading into El Paso. Now the wind lessened, and it became easier to get and hold a compass course. Besides, as we descended I could see the lights of occasional cars on the highway and from ranch houses from time to time on each side of the road. I still had neither navigation nor landing lights on the plane, and the last traces of twilight had become merged in a world of total darkness. Moreover, I reckoned that I was already at least four hours late on the flight plan I had filed in the morning at Dallas. All of this was annoying, but not distressing, as I knew the El Paso airport well and had no fears about landing on the well-lighted runways after dark. One way or the other I would have to set down, and I would just have to wait and see whether or not the airways authorities would take me to task for coming in late and without lights.

The comparatively wide area of illumination that was El Paso was still beyond the horizon; pinpoints of light from ranch houses far below were visible to me as I flew along through the silent, empty night. Now, for the first time since I had fallen in love with flying, I began to wonder if it was worth what it was costing me mentally and physically. Try as I would, I could not shake off such thoughts, and they persisted and grew, interrupted only by our arrival at the El Paso airport, when all of my attention had to be turned toward getting clearance and then landing. But no airways officials berated me; they accepted my explanation about the delay and merely cautioned me to have operating navigation lights before flying again after dark.

It was good to be on the ground again, but I permitted myself to become filled with a resentment which I did not attempt to justify. I reproached myself for not having waited before tackling the pass; I resented the unholy wind for having beaten us unmercifully for hours on end; and, most unreasonable of all, I resented the Aeronca, without which I would not have experienced that nerve-wracking day.

I suddenly decided that I had had enough. I knew there was a train for San Francisco due to depart in about forty minutes and on it I could relax in a warm, comfortable berth, rest my tired eyes and cramped muscles, and let others do the navigating while I rode on to San Francisco without lifting a finger. A call to the railroad station verified the departure time, and I made a Pullman reservation for the train. Then I quickly located an acquaintance who operated a flying service at the airport and told him I was leaving my plane with him to sell for any reasonable offer. It took only a few moments to get my bag from the Aeronca and to be in a taxi on my way to the railway station. I found it difficult to relax and impossible to fight off the heartsickness (I have no other word to describe it) that had begun to gnaw at my insides, but I continued on to the station, jumped out with my small bag, purchased a ticket, and ran down the platform and climbed hurriedly aboard the Pullman.

I didn't even reach my reserved space, for I suddenly became overwhelmed with the heartsickness which previously had only annoyed me. Thoughts of my plane and of my love for flying crowded in upon me, and I said to myself, "Give it up now and you are done with it forever—and you will never forgive yourself." The porter following along behind me still had my bag in his hand. I turned to him with a bill in one hand and the other outstretched for the bag, which I grabbed as I ran past him and on down the vestibule steps as the train began to move. The conductor was just stepping aboard, and

I called out to him, "Lower eight—something has come up, and I'm not going!"

Next morning I was at the airport, bright and early. I told the air service man that I was keeping my plane, and I checked it thoroughly on the ramp. It was in perfect condition—no cracks, dents, or malfunctions anywhere. It had withstood all the buffeting of the past day; only I had succumbed, but now that too was behind me, like an ugly dream. How wonderful it was to rest my hand gently on a sturdy wing and look up at a cloudless sky, knowing that soon the Aeronca and I would be caressed by it and that we would be ready for whatever was in store for us on the way to the Pacific Coast.

The weather was beautiful when we took off and so it continued to Tucson, Yuma, Bakersfield, and, in the late afternoon, the Oakland estuary and landing at what was then called the San Francisco Bay Airdrome at Alameda. The long cross-country flight was over, and in many ways it was one of the most memorable events of my life. I have relived it, in memory, a thousand times.

Before the end of that summer, I was transferred twice—to Los Angeles and then to Butte, Montana. When I arrived at Butte in August, the war clouds in Europe were already lowering. On September 1, I drove up to the curb in front of the Federal building in Billings at about eleven o'clock in the morning and noticed a number of men listening to a radio in a car already parked there. I joined the group and heard the report that Germany had invaded Poland. This meant that World War II was under way. Another agent resided in Billings, and we would go out to his home in the evenings and listen to the war news on his radio. Within a few days the news came through that England and France were in the fight.

Though all of my ancestors came from the British Isles, I had not yet known any of the British and knew of no reason to be acutely disturbed because they were in another war. Yet, I believed them to be in the right; I was single, in good health, could fly airplanes, and I was ready to help if found acceptable. On or about the fifth of September I wrote a letter to the British Consul at San Francisco, assuming he was the nearest representative of that country to Montana, and offered my services as a pilot in the Royal Air Force. A few days later I received a courteous reply from the British consul at Seattle saying that my offer of service had been forwarded to him for reply, that my offer was deeply appreciated, but only citizens of the Commonwealth could be accepted for service. This was changed later, and some Americans were enlisted in the RAF.

There was never a doubt in my mind that this country would eventually become involved in the war; we had once in my lifetime and current events sounded like an old record playing a familiar tune all over again. Therefore, I set about finding the way to be called to active duty under my reserve commission (I had signed up with the Army Reserves in 1929), notwithstanding the fact that I was then forty and only a first lieutenant. If England didn't want me, perhaps my own country did. I wrote to the Bureau, advised them of what I proposed to do and immediately thereafter applied to the Adjutant General for call to active service. It was not forthcoming, not then anyway, and I began a one-man letter-writing campaign which ended only in April, 1942, when I received a call to active duty. By that time, I suppose, the War Department had become finally convinced that I would be less bother in uniform than out of it.

In the meantime, I was assigned to duty with the Bureau in Alaska. In the meantime also, Mammy Callie died. Bill

told me about her last days. They ended as she had lived them
—in peace and quiet, close to one whom she loved and who
loved her in return. One day she closed her eyes, and her heart
just stopped beating. She had already told Bill how she wanted
to be buried: in her newest kerchief, her prettiest dress, and
her "Sunday-go-to-meeting" shoes—and, above all, some member of the family to pray over her. Bill saw to it that these
things were accorded her. Her coffin was brought into Bill's
living room where, amid her friends and loved ones, white
and black, Bill preached her funeral sermon. I was not there
to hear it, but I'm sure that Mammy did in Heaven and very
likely looked down at my brother, a gentle smile on her face,
and said, "Memmie, you is a good man."

Alaska is beautiful—not the warm, sensuous beauty of a
Southern California or Florida, but a stark, cold, and lonely
beauty. In a benign and gentle climate one feels the warm
earth and can touch and smell all that grows upon it. Alaska
is neither intimate nor yielding. The mountains, glaciers,
tundra, and sea seem as distant and unapproachable as the
aurora borealis flooding up and receding in the night sky
along the northern horizon.

Many of the folks in the Territory in those days found a
good portion of their amusement in sustained and diligent
application to the bottle, and they tell a delightful story about
this diversion from the cares of the day. Almost everything
used by the inhabitants was shipped in by boat from Seattle.
The stevedores once went on strike and nothing moved out
to Alaska for months. After a while they got to thinking about
the poor souls in the Territory who, they figured, must be in
dire need of food or even clothes, and relented to the extent
of deciding to load and dispatch one ship to Alaska. But first
they must know what commodity was longed for the most. A

telegram was sent to the suffering populace, saying that one fully loaded ship would be sent and information was needed as to what was wanted most—food, clothes, medicine, or what not. The reply from Alaska was prompt and characteristic: "Keep the food, clothes, medicine, and what not. Send us some whiskey."

My work in the Territory entailed much travel which, if it was between coastal points, was usually made on commercial, or Naval or Coast Guard vessels; but the points in the interior could be reached only by air—military, naval, or commercial —the latter flown by the world-famous "bush pilots."

I made a number of trips to the west—that is to say, the Bering Sea country. All were made in three- or four-passenger planes piloted by bush pilots, and I doubt if any more capable pilots ever existed anywhere. They had to be to survive. Few of the planes had more than one motor and, depending on the season, operated on regular landing gear, floats, or skis. Once away from such centers of population as Juneau, Fairbanks, or Anchorage, there were no real airports, but, instead, relatively short landing strips beside a roadhouse to accommodate the pilot and passengers. These roadhouses were usually two-story wood buildings, having a hallway containing a big stove with a roaring fire to heat the place, a kitchen and dining area below, while upstairs were cots lined along the wall for the weary.

Travel in the winter was an unforgettable experience. The plane would be on skis and one could forget the landing strips if he were flying along one of the major rivers—Yukon, Kuskokwim, or the like—the thickly frozen streams themselves being an almost endless landing surface. During this season each pilot carried his own oil can in his plane, identified with his initials or the identification number of the plane painted on the side. After the plane landed, the passengers would fall to and help the pilot secure it for the night. Iron stakes would be driven into the ice and the plane tied down to them. The engine oil would be drained into the can (otherwise it would freeze during the night) and taken into the roadhouse where it would be set next to the roaring stove.

The next morning (or the next week, depending on the weather) the pilot would take the warm oil out to the plane. A tarpaulin, always kept for that purpose in the plane, would be draped over the engine and cowling, extended in a closed circle down to the ice. In the center of the circle a small gasoline burner would be set off so the hot vapor could envelope the motor. While this was going on the passengers would again lend a hand; one would stand in front of the wing and the other behind. A rope would be thrown across the wing and the two would then begin to whack it smartly up and down across the wing surface to break and knock away the ice that had formed overnight. Having been taught in the States that one courted disaster by leaving a plane exposed to the elements, I was amazed to find that few of the planes in the harsh Alaskan weather ever saw the inside of a hangar, and even more amazed when I realized that they appeared none the worse for it.

My first trip westward was made in the dead of winter in a four-place Bellanca monoplane, whose pilot, I am certain, could have flown it anywhere, anytime, or even blindfolded if he had to. Bad weather set in shortly after we had cleared the mountains to the west of Anchorage and snow was falling heavily. Visibility was reduced to practically zero by the time we reached the landing strip at McGrath. Two planes were on the ground when we landed, and two others came in within a few minutes. This meant that there were about fifteen transients at the small log roadhouse, with nothing to do but wait, eat, sleep, drink, and play poker.

It may have taken as much as ten minutes to get the poker game going; thereafter it ran full blast around the clock. By the second night the snow was deeper, the clouds lower, and my pocketbook gratifyingly thicker. When a man wins oftener than he loses (who could ask for more?) life becomes not only rosy and agreeable, but he is, in a real sense, master of his own movements and actions. He may tell funny stories and laugh gaily at them; he may talk politely to his neighbor, provided that individual's luck has left him in a proper mood for conversation; or he may temporarily quit the wholesome group altogether. The man who is being frowned on by Lady Luck is in a different category, for while ill fortune may have cracked his skull until he becomes suspicious of every hand dealt to him and his hope of eventual victory is not overwhelming, still he knows that although he may continue to lose by playing, he is certain not to recoup if he stops. So he bends rigidly over the table of chance in agonizing anticipation, laughing at no jokes and telling no tales. Perhaps from such situations as this came the old poker saw: "The winners —they tell funny stories, while the losers—they yell 'DEAL'!"

Since I then found myself happily in the first category I experienced no pangs of conscience when I decided to be done with the game for a while and seek a little fresh air (I had encountered none in some thirty-six hours running). The snow was too deep to walk very far, and I certainly did not intend to run the risk of cutting my current invisible ties with Lady Luck by staying out of the game for an extended period, especially since I had just won a sizable pot (the game was no limit) with a trifling hand that contained only two queens and three other cards that added nothing to the little value it possessed before the draw. When a man can win in such a game with such a hand, he is indeed holding it with one hand while the other is wrist deep in a gold mine.

I made a circle of the roadhouse and came on a low, square log building just to the rear, made visible by a light shining through a window of the house. As I trudged silently by it in the deep snow I heard a sound from within, so unexpected and so long unheard that it did not register on my memory until I had reached the far end of the roadhouse. I came to an abrupt halt when the realization dawned on me that what I had just heard sounded exactly like a cow. Then I reflected that such was impossible, for a cow had no more business in McGrath than an Eskimo in the Congo. I could think of no way by which a cow could be got to McGrath, for it was surrounded for many miles in all directions by highwayless, railroadless, and oceanless tundra and forests. Even conceding that a cow somewhere, sometime had heard of McGrath and just decided to trek to it from its native habitat, I seriously doubted if one could live long enough to accomplish the feat, surely not alone, and surely there would not be two or more crazy enough to try it at the same time.

Even so, a man from Mississippi should recognize a cow when he hears one. I turned and retraced my steps to the shed. The door was secured by a padlock, which I rattled as vigorously as my cold hands would permit. First I could hear some shuffling sort of noise, followed immediately by the same sound I had heard before. It was still exactly like a cow, and I still did not believe it.

I went back to the poker table to settle the matter once and for all by asking the roadhouse proprietor to tell me what was in the shed. But I found that by then he had run into a disastrous string of five straight bets into one card draws, the outrageous proportion of four having been made. This meant that by this time he had unhappily joined the agonized ranks of the wretches who were yelling, "Deal."

A man who sets some value on his own precious hide does

well to give serious thought to the possible consequences resulting from injecting extraneous matter into the attention of a loser in a game of chance. So I deferred and tried to take the edge off my curiosity by the thought that, for all I knew, every roadhouse in the Territory had a shed behind in which reposed an animal that said "moo" just like a Mississippi cow.

It was not until three days later, when the ceiling had lifted to a thousand feet and we were ready to take off, that I asked the proprietor of the roadhouse what it was that sounded like a cow in his shed. The players were clearing out, and he was still loser, and conversation did not come easy or urbane. He said, "It's a cow." But I was still curious—how did he get it to McGrath? The nearest place where cows were known to reside was away across the forbidding mountains, over which even a mountain goat would find the going tough; a boat could not come within two hundred, or a train or truck within five hundred miles. He must have figured that my interest was genuine, for he added that, next to good whiskey, milk was his favorite drink and, having done better in a poker game two years ago than in the disaster he had just attended, he chartered an old Ford tri-motor and flew the beast in from Seattle. It must have cost him a pretty penny.

There was an investigation to be made at a small village on the Bering Sea, not far from the Arctic Circle. Again it was winter, and I was traveling with the same pilot in the old Bellanca. By the time we had made half the distance from Anchorage, the other two passengers had been deposited at their respective destinations, and only the pilot and I were left for the remainder of the trip. The Yukon River was being used as a landing strip, and the pilot would radio ahead his next port of call in order that a citizen of the community could go to the river, check it for obstructions, then remain on hand to indicate to the pilot the best place to set down on the frozen river. Our destination came into view late in the afternoon, low on the cold, grey horizon—a few snow-covered huts here and there along the river bank and the Bering Sea just beyond. We came in at less than a hundred feet altitude and quickly saw a native in parka and mukluks standing on the ice about twenty feet offshore. He first swung his arm to indicate the wind direction, then pointed at the surface just to his left to show the best point for touch down. On the bank were his dog team and sled. The place of landing was about three miles from the settlement, and we went to it on the sled. This was my first venture in such a vehicle, and it was not an auspicious one either, for we had not gone more than a mile or so when suddenly a big moose crossed the path in front of us. The lead dog took off after him without hesitation and the others followed, promptly tipping over the sled, and out we went in the deep snow.

The next morning I set out on the business that had brought me to this tiny settlement at the end of nowhere. As I trudged through the snow drifts along the one and only path in town, I lost my footing on a slight incline and slithered over against a weatherbeaten, ice-covered log hut. When I picked myself up I noticed that the door to the hut was partially open because of the thick ice at the base of it. I glanced inside and almost tumbled over again, this time in astonishment, for there was an automobile, or rather what was left of one. This was almost as incredible as the cow at McGrath, perhaps even more so, because the cow was useful, but there was no place one could drive an automobile within hundreds of miles of the settlement, so remote that it could be reached only by boat in the summer or air in the winter.

I squeezed through the partly open door and gaped at the dilapidated skeleton of an automobile. It was a 1923 model Chevrolet coupe, and when I rested a hand on one of the two remaining fenders, it promptly dropped off onto the earthen floor. The seat cushions had become lumps of yellowish flakes; the tires had long since rotted off and were now nothing more than small mounds of brittle rubber covering each rim where it touched the floor; the glassless windshield frame had toppled over and lay across the hood. The car must have had a metal top at one time, but there remained only several pieces of rusty tin hanging from two brittle and rusty arches. No trace of paint remained on the vehicle, only the accumulated, unmolested rust of eighteen years. I wondered who could have contrived to get it there in the first place, how he could have managed it, and, above all, what he had intended to do with it.

Some oldtime residents knew the story and gave me the details. It could have happened only in Alaska and is so charming as to make it a tale to be treasured. Here it is as related to me:

A local miner struck it rich near Fairbanks in 1921 or 1922 and then returned to this, his native settlement, to rest, take it easy, and spend his money. He had never seen an automobile, but somehow or other he happened upon a Chevrolet catalogue. The picture of the coupe intrigued him, and, having ample funds to satisfy his desire, he ordered one, just the way he would send off for long-handled winter underwear or a Gramophone. The only means by which the car could be shipped was by train to the West Coast, by ocean-going vessel to a port of entry in Alaska or Canada, then by river boat for hundreds of miles down the Yukon, navigable only during the summer. The factory received his order too late to get the car to the river boat before the annual freeze, so delivery had to be held up until the following year's thaw. All told, it was something like ten or twelve months before the river boat with the shiny new coupe arrived at the settlement, but the cargo could not be discharged until the next high tide. It then developed that the boat could not be gotten near enough to the shore to set the little coupe on dry land. So the miner, with the willing assistance of his neighbors, set up four stilts right in front of his cabin, which was situated on what later became a little island just offshore at high tide. Now there was something solid to hold up the coupe and keep it from being dumped into twenty or twenty-five feet of water.

The shiny vehicle was hoisted off the boat and onto the stilts. The boat gave a farewell toot and went on about its business. So the miner had his pretty coupe, lacked only a place to drive it, a way to get it down off the stilts, and some gasoline and oil to use in getting the motor to run. No one else in the settlement had ever seen an automobile either, so the question might well be open to some reasonable doubt that any of them could have accomplished much toward activating the coupe even if there had been gasoline and a place to drive it.

However, neither a road nor fuel was needed immediately, as a number of years passed before they even began to figure some way to get it down off the stilts. In the meantime, the boats continued to make their long and desolate way downriver each summer and, until they reached the settlement, no one aboard had ever seen a coupe on stilts. When a boat chugged into the view the old miner was sitting in the car atop the stilts, a crock of good drinking whiskey in one hand and the other pressing the horn button. When the boat drew abreast he honked the horn and the boat answered him. Of course, the battery gave out before very long. Thereafter he could still sit on the stilts, but he could only wave at the astonished folk on the passing boats. The summer sun and winter ice bore down on the car during the passing years, and by the time it was finally got down and into the log shed there remained little more than a shell of the once bright and shiny automobile.

No one that I questioned could recall what became of the old miner, but each was certain that the automobile had never been driven a foot.

I was in Anchorage that Sunday in 1941 when we found ourselves at war. Anchorage is close to the same longitude as Hawaii, thus in the same time zone, and the attack at Pearl Harbor was still under way when the news of it was received in Alaska. Though we had frequently talked of the probability of war with Japan, I doubt if the thought had ever occurred to anyone that she would even consider a surprise attack on a place as far away as Hawaii. I wondered as I hurried into my clothes if an attack would be made on Elmendorf Field as well. After all, it was no more distant from Japan than Pearl Harbor and had by now become a base of considerable proportions. General Buckner must have had the same idea, for I could see fighter-plane cover overhead as soon as I stepped out of my hotel.

For more than a year we had been carefully checking the activities and exact whereabouts of all Japanese, German, and Italian nationals (or extractions) residing in the far reaches of the Territory; all plans had been made to place certain of them in immediate custody in the event of war. So, with the military, we set about to get those listed rounded up. In the meantime, of course, every time someone lit a cigar in the open at night or cranked his outboard motor another spy report was rushed to the office. During the next several days I had little opportunity to think of personal affairs, and even less to act on them. Thus, almost a week had passed after Pearl Harbor before I was able to get to my office about three o'clock one morning and get off another request for call to active duty, now that we were at war.

Two days later, long before my letter could have reached Washington, an acquaintance in the Army Signal Corps office called to me as I was hurrying down the corridor in the Federal Building. He handed me a cablegram from the War Department which had just come in. I opened the envelope without delay. The cable was addressed to me by my military title and signed by no less than the Secretary of War Mr. Simpson. This was wonderful, I thought, I was not only getting action but from the head man himself. It proposed an action all right, but hardly the sort I had yearned for. The Secretary had been in conference with the director of the FBI concerning the ninety-two members of that organization who held reserve commissions, and it had been decided that, because of our civilian duties, none would be called to active duty, and, further, to assure that such could not take place, each of us was requested to resign his commission immediately.

This was a blow, disheartening and totally unexpected as far as I was concerned. I was a thousand miles away from my headquarters city, Juneau, and five thousand from Bureau headquarters at Washington, and thus had no idea what the others faced with the situation were going to do about it. But as for myself, it was as simple as it had always been. My first duty was to the military service, now more than ever.

Again I sat down at my typewriter and wrote out a reply to the cablegram, setting forth my basic feeling that as a citizen my duty to my country forced me to respectfully decline to submit my resignation from the armed services in time of war, and that I was again requesting immediate call to active duty. I addressed my reply to the Secretary of War. I knew that I had much on my side, for I had never heard of an officer, reserve or otherwise, being forced out of military service unless his activities merited expulsion, whereas my military record was good, as was my health, and I had already served in one war before I ever heard of the FBI. I went even further; I requested a definite foreign assignment on being called to active duty. To those of us in faraway Alaska at that time the war in Europe was considered as very nearly on another planet, but the Pacific was, in a sense, our beat, and it was there that we had been attacked. This led me to request that I be assigned to a unit in the Philippines. Of course, I later thanked my lucky stars that this part of the request was not granted; otherwise I would surely have spent a good part of the war as a Japanese prisoner, if indeed I had survived.

At the same time I sent an airmail letter to the Bureau explaining what steps I had taken and why.

Not being privy to what went on in the office of the Secretary of War, I have no way of knowing whether he ever personally saw or concerned himself with my reply. But someone did, and whoever it was knew that my refusal to quit the reserve was based on solid ground. It put them on the spot, and there was one infallible way to get off—order me to active duty.

The long-awaited orders placing me on extended active military duty reached me in April, 1942. I was to report to the Counter Intelligence Corps at Washington on May 11. I went back to Juneau, left all my official files at the office, and got a ride to the outside (Seattle) in a military C-47 transport. I proceeded to the local FBI office and turned in all my FBI equipment, then went to a military supply store where I bought uniforms and insignias, afterwards packing my civilian clothing into a trunk and shipping it to Mother at Oxford to keep for me until the war would be over.

12 THERE WAS ANOTHER WAR

A T LONG LAST I WAS IN UNIFORM. MY MILITARY SERVICE
would take me halfway around the world. I would see
new countries and strange people, get promoted twice, be
refused action as a military pilot a dozen times, learn enough
of a foreign language to understand others and make myself
understood, manage to get myself shot at again, and marry
the prettiest blonde in all Africa.

When I reported for duty in Washington, I requested assignment to the Air Force with the view of acquiring pilot
status but was turned down—too old. Then I requested overseas duty and was more fortunate; I was assigned without
delay to the first counter intelligence unit then being readied

for dispatch to the European theater of operations. The commander of the CIC detachment to which I was assigned was Captain Kirby Gillette, a Texan and a former FBI agent. He had resigned in 1940 and was called up under his reserve commission a short time later.

We embarked at the port of New York on a converted English passenger vessel and crossed the Atlantic as part of a tremendous convoy, the sea being covered with parallel lines of ships as far as the eye could see. After the war I read that more Allied vessels were sunk during the month of June, 1942, than at any other period during the entire war; that was when we crossed, but we never heard a shot fired.

We landed at Belfast, spent the night in an Irish barracks, and early the next morning marched back to the quay to board a cross-channel vessel for Scotland. Our knapsacks were strapped to our backs, and most of us, including myself, had our names stenciled across them. Local residents lined each side of the approach route and called or waved to us as we filed slowly past. Three elderly men were bending over and looking at the names as we passed them. When I came abreast of them I heard one say, "Ah, 'tis a Falkner no less." Then one called out, "Welcome home, me lad!" It was a surprise. Although I had not considered the name "Falkner" as Irish, I did have some Clarks and Swifts in my ancestry; so, with them in mind, I saluted the gentlemen and expressed my appreciation.

But within a short time I was going to have to call on the McAlpins, Deans, and Murrys in the family tree, for almost as soon as I had set foot on the soil of Scotland I noticed a man wearing a blue uniform who, like the Irish across the channel, was looking intently at the names on our knapsacks. When he made out mine he snapped to a sort of semi-attention, rendered a smart salute, and said, "Welcome home, Captain

Falkner!" This was another pleasant surprise, especially coming so quickly after the first, but was worthy of even greater appreciation, for the Scot had misread my insignia and advanced me from lowly lieutenant to exalted captain.

We went by troop train to Cheltenham, then a few weeks later to London, where I was assigned to the Allied Headquarters in Grosvenor Square. Company-grade officers are not usually privy to momentous events in the making, but we could see that something big was in the air. One day when I had occasion to be the bearer of some official papers marked "Top Secret" to the office of our commanding officer, a British colonel, I took the liberty of remarking to him that there seemed to be something in the offing, which I figured could only mean an invasion somewhere, and that, when it came, I would like to be in on it. He looked at me, smiled, and said, "I think you'll do. Sit tight and you'll hear from me."

He was true to his word. Two days later he sent for me. He told me that the proposed operation had the code name of "Torch" and would involve the invasion of North Africa by Allied forces in either October or November and that, as requested, I was being assigned to the intelligence unit. In the meantime I was to mention the matter to no one.

In the latter part of October I got my sealed orders, naming me as commander of the CIC detachment assigned to the center task force which would go ashore at Oran, Algeria. The next day I was promoted to captain, and the next week I was with my detachment on a troop train that arrived at Glennock, Scotland. The boat convoy was riding at anchor offshore, and the troops were ferried out to it by lighters. Ours was under the command of a British lieutenant. A sheet of paper in his hand, he looked closely at the names on the vessels as we maneuvered between them and finally pointed to a big troop ship and told me this was the one which would take us aboard. As we passed slowly under the vessel's stern I looked up at the name, the S.S. *Mariposa*. I recognized it at once as being the Lurline ship on which I had made a security investigation at Long Beach, California, in 1939; now I was to ride it as part of an invasion force headed for North Africa.

The first echelon of the task force was already ashore when we entered the harbor at Mers-el-Kebir (Oran), which was filled with masts and funnels of sunken ships, military and civilian. Debarkment was uneventful, with only a few pot-shots from snipers here and there. Nights were different; there was a lot of shipping, and Axis bombers wasted no time attack-ing ships and docks. During these periods the antiaircraft defenses which ringed the inner harbor put on spectacular displays of firepower.

I set up shop on the upper floor of an office building down-town and went to work, running down the remaining mem-bers of the Axis control commission still in the territory, their cohorts, and their military supplies.

After the French had come over to join us in the efforts against their former masters I had an extremely interesting visitor at the office. He wore the uniform and insignia of a captain of the French Foreign Legion, and when he ap-peared before me I addressed him in my halting French. He smiled and replied in pure, unadulterated, midwestern United States English. We talked at length, and he told me a rare story. He was a native of Kentucky and had resided there, in Illinois, and in Ohio. In his early twenties he became restless and decided, just like that, to join the Legion. He worked his way to North Africa in 1928 and landed with his pockets empty but his determination to enlist in the Legion undiminished. He was immediately accepted for a five-year hitch in the corps. He liked the lonely and dangerous life and advanced through the enlisted grades. He received several citations for valor and, in some minute and (outside the Corps) unheard-of campaign against the Arabs deep in the Sahara Desert, was awarded a battlefield commission, later advancing to his current grade of captain. He concluded by saying that he was then assigned to the famous headquarters of the Corps at Sidi-bel-Abbes, only about seventy kilometers away, and that I was cordially invited to visit if and when I could get time off.

Thoughts of the Kentucky Foreign Legion captain left me until one evening two weeks later when I was partaking of some native wine in a local bistro with an acquaintance, a captain in a nearby antiaircraft battery. I learned that he, too, had read *Beau Geste,* had never forgotten it, and harbored a strong desire to see the renowned Sidi-bel-Abbes. I mentioned my visitor, and the captain expressed immediate interest and the hope that we could find some way to accept the invitation I had received. At mess the same evening my commanding officer mentioned that he was thinking of sending an officer to call on the commander of the Foreign Legion as a goodwill gesture. I promptly offered my services and he as promptly accepted them, telling me to get a unit jeep and proceed to Sidi-bel-Abbes the following day. I called the antiaircraft captain, who was not only enthusiastic over the prospect but was his own boss as well and was free to go.

We arrived at the Corps headquarters before noon. I never saw a place that so accurately and precisely fit what I had imagined it to be. It was like returning to a place visited years before. The village itself consisted of a few white, stone buildings in the center and elsewhere of mud huts set among the date palms and olive trees. The compact base of the Legion adjoined the southern edge of the town; entry to it was by way of a big, swinging gate where sentries were on constant duty.

When we told a sentry we wished to speak to the commanding officer, he called a turbaned sergeant major, who escorted us to the headquarters building and ushered us into the presence of a French regular army colonel. He spoke some English and we had a pleasant visit; we were particularly delighted when he offered to have his adjutant accompany us on a tour of the whole base. As we were preparing to leave his office with the adjutant, he asked us to wait a moment, then reached into a drawer and picked up two small insignias of the Sixth Regiment of the Legion. He pinned one on each of us and pronounced us honorary members of the regiment. It was a proud distinction, and I brought the pin home with me, gave it to Mother, and she kept it among my souvenirs of the two wars.

The war moved on to Tunisia, and I badgered the Air Corps for a transfer there and an assignment to fly military aircraft—any sort, anywhere, anytime. Finally, after persistent pestering, I was authorized to take a flight physical examination. The idea was, I suppose, that no man of forty-three could hope to pass it and thereafter I would be off their backs. They were properly astounded when the military doctors found me physically qualified to fly, but were still individually determined not to be the ones to set me out on such a course.

This convinced me at last that whatever part I was to take in war, it would be with at least one foot on the ground. In the spring of 1943 I was transferred to the Allied Supreme Headquarters in Algiers, the largest city I had yet seen in Africa. The wide, paved streets were lined with trees and flowers; there were fine public buildings and residences in the European sections, but only dark hovels lining narrow, winding alleyways in the native quarters, especially in the Casbah, into which unattractive den I had to go several times. It was at once sinister and repulsive; lean and hungry animals and silent, robed and turbaned humans spilled in and out, flowing relentlessly along the dank and dismal alleys. The atmosphere was evil and the odor a stinking curse.

The American Red Cross in Algiers, as was the case everywhere I saw it in operation, did much to improve the lot of the servicemen. It aided them in communicating with home and with other servicemen, and it furnished a place for them to bathe and change clothes when they could find the time. It also arranged in Algiers for local entertainers, dancers, musicians, and the like to perform in military hospitals and nearby bases. One evening I attended a ballet (I never saw another and have no idea to this day why I went to see this one), and one member of it was as attractive as any young woman I had ever seen. She was pure blonde and, while such are not unknown among the French, still one does not usually associate them with the general population of France. She was certainly of European stock and, I thought, probably of Scandinavian or Teutonic origin, but in either case it appeared inconceivable that she could be in a country where exit and entry for civilians were practically impossible during the war years.

I managed to meet her and found that while from the audience she was singularly attractive, close up she was beautiful. She told me about herself. Her father, then dead, was an adventurous individual in his own right. After finishing military school and being commissioned in his native France, he was posted to duty in Algeria, liked the country, and stayed on. His daughter had been born in Constantine, Algeria. He went back to France with his battalion of Spahis at the beginning of World War I, was gravely wounded at Verdun in 1916, and became a prisoner of war. German military doctors saved his life. He recovered from his wounds and was released from captivity in 1918 after the armistice, thereafter returning to duty in North Africa. He received the French Legion of Honor during World War I and the rarely awarded medal of valor known as the "Ouicham Alouid" for his part in the desert warfare against the infamous Abdel Krim in the 1920's.

In August, 1943, I was promoted to major and assigned to setting up security detachments at the military air bases across the northern rim of the continent and on into Italy, from Marrakech to Casablanca to Sfax in Tunisia, on to the islands of Sardinia and Sicily, and across the Italian boot to Bari on the Adriatic. This put me on the go almost constantly.

As she always did when any of us were away from home, Mother wrote to me regularly. She told me that Bill's efforts to get into military service had been unavailing, that John had been commissioned in the Navy and was on active duty, as was our cousin, John, Jr., and that John's eldest son Jimmy had completed naval flight training at Pensacola, received his commission, and had applied for and been assigned to duty as a pilot in the U.S. Marine Corps. He was then nineteen.

By the fall of 1943 the war had moved on, and the continent of Africa was being used only as a supply and staging area for further assaults on some of the Mediterranean islands and the European mainland. Security measures were tight, but because of the nature of my assignments the Allied Headquarters in Algiers had issued to me what was known as a Number One, Top Priority Identification Card, by means of which I could go anywhere in the theater at any time by any available means of transportation; it also authorized me to be privy to any military plans and dispositions.

On my return to Algiers from Casablanca in April, 1944, I was told that the French, acting alone, had made an unsuccessful amphibious assault on the island of Elba, held by the Germans for more than a year; and that another assault had

been authorized, but only after we were certain that the
French had all the supplies and troops needed to assure the
success of the venture. I was assigned, with a British colonel,
as liaison with the French on the island of Corsica, from which
the invasion of Elba would be launched. We proceeded at
once to Ajaccio, Corsica, held numerous conferences with the
French command, ascertained what would be needed, and
arranged to have it supplied without delay.

Military supplies for the French arrived almost daily, as
did regular army units as reinforcements, consisting of Sene-
galese, Spahis, and Tauregs from all over North Africa. Arrangements were made for combat units of the British navy
to furnish support cover for the attack force and for American
landing craft to transport the troops and equipment to the
beachheads. The date for the attack was June 22, 1944. The
British colonel with whom I was working, in a little room at
the Ajaccio grammar school, casually remarked to me the day
before the invasion that we were our own bosses and therefore free to come and go as we wished. I didn't know what he
was getting at, but then he told me what he had in mind—why
not assign ourselves to the invasion force and go along with
it? Why not indeed? thought I, for here at last was a ready-
made chance to see what made the war tick. We agreed that
we wouldn't even need written orders; all we had to do was
be aboard a landing craft when it cast off.

The landing craft were assembled and being loaded in a
bay across the island, and we had just time to make the trip
in our trusty jeep. The colonel, like myself, had one of the
top priority cards. We arrived at the bay shortly before midnight, boarded the first landing craft we saw that was still
tied up at the jetty, and went topside to identify ourselves to
the commanding officer. The assault troops, consisting of one
company of Spahis and one of Tauregs (all officers were

French), were already aboard. The landing craft and support vessels were of course in total darkness and continued under blackout restrictions as the convoy and escort vessels lined up and set course for the nearby island of Elba.

An infantry landing craft has a big, mouth-like door in the bow which is lowered from the top to a position parallel with the deck as a sort of extended bridge by which the debarking troops can get from the vessel to the shore. We stayed on the small, circular bridge with the ship's commander, who told us that his boat was to be second in line going into the center beach. The sea was running in gentle swells, there was little wind, and the night was light enough so that the nearby vessels in the columns to starboard and port could be seen riding the restless sea up and down as they pushed steadily forward. The three of us talked intermittently of the war, the colonel of his home in England, the lieutenant of his in Illinois, and I of mine in Mississippi; for the most part we looked silently ahead through the encompassing and silent night.

On the open deck immediately below the bridge the troops sat shoulder to shoulder awaiting, as any soldier does in the hours preceding battle, what the morrow would bring. From time to time, above the muffled exhaust of the motors and the soft thud of the flat bow as it met another swell head on, one could hear snatches of conversation in French or some desert dialect; otherwise the restless, rolling sea was enveloped in silence and darkness.

The still hours passed, and almost imperceptibly came the realization that the dawn of another day was riding along the horizon directly forward. Now we could see the support vessels—a British gunboat close in and half way down the starboard column and two corvettes close in and abeam of the lead ship in the port column. Then, dead ahead, we could make out the hilly outline of our destination, the island of

Elba, becoming ever more sharply outlined against the break-ing day that was sweeping away the night from the sea.

The officer in charge of the whole operation was a British admiral in the gunboat, and orders came through from him by radio for the assault vessels to properly space themselves and be prepared on command to shove forward to their re-spective beaching areas, discharge the troops, and get back out of gunfire from the shore as quickly as possible. The three columns of assault vessels jockeyed into the designated align-ment, and orders came for them to proceed toward the nearby beaches at half speed; the escort vessels were to begin bom-barding the shore on signal from the gunboat. A few moments later a greenish-white star shell spurted skyward from the gun-boat; then the corvettes too began shelling the beaches and, I suppose, as far inland as their weapons would reach.

Retaliation from the German batteries ashore was immedi-ate and accurate. We could see flashes from gun emplacements just inland from the shore, and mortar and artillery shells whistled all around. The landing craft directly in front of us took several hits from what must have been among the first salvos from the shore. Fire broke out upon it, and the vessel stopped dead in the water and slowly swung broadside toward us. Another craft to starboard was also afire and apparently out of control. Our ship commander gave a series of rapid orders, just in time to get his craft off a collision course with the helpless and flaming boat in front of us. As soon as we had cleared the burning boat and turned back on course toward the beach, the lieutenant called out to me that we would hit the beach dead ahead and that the commanding officer of the French troops should have his men ready to scramble off the craft as soon as he got it as near shore as he could. On the deck below the troops were lined up in battle gear behind their French officers. I scurried down to give the lieutenant's message to the commanding officer of the troops, a French major as calm and self-assured as if he were getting ready for a parade back at Sidi-bel-Abbes. He gravely saluted me and said that he and his troops would quit the vessel as soon as the landing gate was lowered.

I hurried back to the bridge, where the lieutenant had out his binoculars and was closely scanning the shore, now only a few boat lengths away. As he could see no way to maneuver directly onto the beach, he made a quick decision. As soon as he was certain the water would not be over our heads, he would hold the vessel as steady as possible, have the gate dropped, and hope we could clear the ship in time for him to back away, turn, and get the hell out before his boat met the same fate as some of the others. The British colonel and I quickly thanked the young lieutenant for the ride and wished him luck in getting his ship away from the beach and beyond the range of enemy fire. He replied, "I'm sure going to try. As soon as the last Arab is in the drink I'm getting the hell out of here." Then he hesitated a second and added, "I don't envy you two—I'll take my chance with the boat any day."

The British colonel and I dropped down from the bridge and squirmed our way through the mass of silent, motionless Arabs and on up to a position beside the French major just inside the bow gate. From this position we could no longer see the land or anything upon the sea, but we could hear the enemy shelling as intense as ever. In a few moments the exhaust from the motors abruptly ceased, and the ship was rocking gently on the inshore swells. Then there was a dull crunch on the starboard hull and the lieutenant called down from the bridge, "This is it—good luck!" The big chains rattled as the gate thumped down and outward. The beach was directly ahead, but separated from us by about twenty feet of pure Mediterranean Sea. The French major held up a hand and shouted, "En avant mes enfants!"

There was just time for us to jerk our pistols from their holsters and hold them high over our heads as we slid down into the water up to our chests. Bullets were thudding against the hull of the vessel and making small geysers erupt in the water, and I thought as we sloshed on to the shore that here I was, after twenty-six years, again being shot at by the same people in the same general corner of the world. As the African troops stepped out of the water the French officers motioned them into position and within a few moments all were moving up the first hill in line of attack. Some were hit by mortar fire as we crossed the open beach; the others continued on with the French major a few paces in front, his service pistol in one hand and a swagger stick in the other. The thought came to me as I watched him that no matter how courageous the gesture, it was certainly one that was vanishing from any battlefield.

This time the assault was a complete success; the entire island was secured and all the enemy either killed or made prisoner by noon of the following day. It was, I believe, the last Mediterranean island held by the Germans during the war and with this attack they had been cleared from all of them.

Having traveled throughout the North African theater of operations for months on end, I had come by the means of setting up my own private communication system, which served me well in connection with the pretty blonde back in Algiers, in whose clear blue eyes I had, somehow or other, found favor. I got word to her after the invasion on Elba that I would return to Algiers in August, 1944, and hoped that she would marry me then. The word she sent back was, "yes."

We were actually married twice in Algiers, first by an army chaplain and afterward by the mayor of the town. Then I returned to my affairs in connection with the war effort, and it was agreed that she would come to the United States when I could arrange it.

I was transferred back to the States on rotation, and my wife joined me in 1945. When I introduced people to Suzanne, they realized as soon as she spoke that she was neither born nor brought up hereabouts. The natural question then followed, "Where are you from?" In the beginning I would reply for her that she was from Africa, which is, of course, the literal truth. But it invariably brought on a certain, definite perplexity, for the questioner would then again carefully note her blue eyes, blonde hair, and fair complexion, and stare at me with unconcealed disbelief. The trouble is that anyone seeing her finds it difficult or impossible to believe that she could be a native of a country whose population is almost universally believed to have physical attributes completely opposed to hers. Finally we both gave up, made no further reference to Africa, and simply contented ourselves and the questioners, I hope, with the statement that she is French, which is just as true but not so perplexing.

After I returned home from North Africa I was assigned to the Pentagon, where I remained on duty more than a year and got lost in the endless corridors at least once every day. In the meantime, John had been in a serious jeep accident while on Navy duty and was in traction at a naval hospital; the doctors held little hope that we would be able to quit them for months. His son Jimmy was a second lieutenant with a Marine squadron in the Pacific flying land-based Corsairs. His plane was shot down at sea while he was returning from a raid on the Japanese mainland, but he had the good fortune to be rescued by one of our destroyers. He served with distinction, gaining several military medals and bringing much honor to himself and the family name.

In 1946 John received a total medical discharge. The jeep wreck very nearly took his life. He never complained, but it was easy to see that he suffered. I was at home in 1958 on a visit and asked him if he was ever completely free from pain. He replied, "Rarely," and changed the subject.

The date of my release from active duty was set for June 30, 1946, and as soon as I got the notice I called Mr. Hoover's office and was given an appointment to see him the following day. He received me graciously, as he always did, and I told him I would be ready to go back to work in July. He asked if I had a preference as to office of assignment. I did, and asked to be sent to Los Angeles, having in mind the soft ocean breezes and the date palms there, compared with some cold and windswept days I had spent on the Mediterranean and in Italy during the war. I shed my uniform on discharge and took up my life in the FBI again. In some ways it seemed as foreign as some of the countries I had visited overseas, and in others as though I had never left it at all.

13 THREE SCORE AND TEN, MORE AND LESS

THE "BIG WAR" WAS OVER. BACK HOME AND IN CIVILIAN clothes were the members of the family who had taken part in it—John, Jimmy, our cousin Lieutenant John W. T. Falkner IV, and me. Home to the others was still Oxford. Mine would be wherever the FBI sent me. Something else was also over for my brothers Bill and John and me: our final hold on youth, the greatest prize of all, the one easiest acquired—one needs only to be born—and easiest lost—one needs only to live.

In the fall of 1946 I was transferred to New Orleans and my wife and I remained there for almost eight years, during which time we made frequent trips back to Oxford. One day, with

Mother, we drove to Ripley to revisit the old familiar scenes of long ago and for Mother and me to show Suzanne where the family first took root in Mississippi. At that time the Old Colonel's home still stood, with its pointed domes and heavy wood- and metal-work. Great-grandfather had seen this architectural adornment while touring Europe after his railroad began to prosper, liked the designs, and had them incorporated into his own home then being constructed at Ripley.

We drove out to the cemetery where Falkners and Murrys rest, the Old Colonel's statute rising high and unmistakable above the plot. We continued on for a few miles north of town to the village of Falkner, Mississippi, and I thought that if there is any validity in the old adage about the overwhelming advantage of being a big fish in a little pond, rather than the other way around, I should be done with roaming some fine day, return to this little settlement, pitch a tent, and live out my remaining years. But these are things of which dreams are made: dreams they were and dreams they remain, for I have never returned to this quiet land of my ancestors.

It was during this period that total recognition came to Bill as a writer, honors being heaped on him from every quarter, including the highest, The Nobel Prize in Literature. But none of it changed him to the slightest extent. His only child Jill married a young man of Washington, D.C., Paul Summers, and they went to Charlottesville, Virginia, to live. Bill accepted a position as Writer in Residence at the University of Virginia in the same city. He soon obtained what amounted to a second home, and he and Estelle took up part-time residence there. I say "part-time," because Oxford was still, and always would be, "home" to him, and he then sort of commuted between Mississippi and Virginia.

John was living at Oxford during this time, and Bill was usually there when Suzanne and I returned to visit the family.

We always stayed at Mother's home, and after our arrival she would call Bill and John and they would usually come by every day to visit. In the summer, and at other times if the weather was good, we would all sit on the porch. We talked of many things: of our youth in Oxford and of the earlier days of the family in Tippah County; of hunting and fishing in the fields and streams which we knew as well as Mother's front yard; of books we had all known and loved; and, finally, of how certain we were that the new generation of Falkners—Jimmy, Chooky, Jill, and Dean—would bring honor and respect to our name.

By the late 1950's the time had come for my brothers and me, as it must for all, to reflect on the future, not with the zest of youth to whom tomorrow is but another day and those remaining seem endless, but with the quiet and numbing realization that the end we could once ignore was now too near to avoid contemplation. During these years Mother spoke not infrequently of the hereafter, Bill rarely, and John never.

In spite of repeated entreaties by Bill and John, who I am sure were joined by Estelle and Lucille, Mother declined to live anywhere but in her home. In October, 1960, she was found unconscious on the floor of her bedroom and was taken immediately to the Oxford Hospital. Jimmy called me, and, when I got to Oxford, she was still in a coma. Her doctor said she could not emerge and would be dead within a week.

Some members of the family were always at the hospital, none more often than Jimmy and Chookie and their wives. I had just come from Mother's room early one morning and was sitting alone on the steps at the front of the building when Bill drove up in his little red station wagon. He approached me and, knowing that any change in Mother could only be for the worse, simply said, "Let's go in and see Mother." We remained at her bedside for ten or fifteen minutes, then went back outside and sat down together on the concrete steps. It was a clear fall day and people of the community were going placidly about their affairs; only Mother inside on the hospital bed was motionless, except for her breathing which seemed to become more labored with each passing day.

Bill got out his pipe, slowly filled the bowl with the special tobacco which was blended for him in London, and fished a big kitchen match from a pocket of his ancient hunting jacket. Then, with unlit pipe in one hand and unstruck match in the other, he gazed out at the unhurried traffic and asked me what my thoughts were on the hereafter. I carefully explained them as best I could, and when I had finished he struck the match on the concrete and applied the swelling flame to his pipe. It didn't catch very well, and I remember he took the pipe from his mouth and gently tapped the bowl on the step; then, gazing again across the now empty street, he said, "Maybe each of us will become some sort of radio wave."

Mother passed away in the early morning hours of October 21, 1960. Bill and John and I returned to her room and one after the other, in the order in which she had given us life, we leaned over the bed and for the last time kissed the dear forehead in death as each had done so often in life.

Mother had told each of us repeatedly that she wanted to be buried in the family plot near Dean and with as little delay as possible. We carried out her wishes.

I went back to the family home: There was her easel with an unfinished oil painting upon it; there were her books, pamphlets, and newspapers in orderly array, family paintings and photographs on the walls and tables, and close beside her bed Mammy's small and ancient, but still sturdy rocking chair. And I thought of how Mother, in common with the rest of us, never ceased to remember Mammy. Now both were gone forever; only the rocking chair remained.

Mother lived to see her eldest son gain every honor that

could come to a man of letters. John, too, had been published many times. She was not given to expressing her emotions a great deal, but it was easily apparent that she was very proud of them both. I've heard her say that she thought John deserved more recognition than he got, and that Bill would have had very little had he depended on the people in our county for it. Perhaps that is the reason she felt so grateful to those who did go out of their way to speak with pride of this native son.

As was inevitable, once we arrived at manhood, many of Bill's interests and mine ceased to be the same. He had his life to live and I, mine. He had lived in New Orleans and had been abroad during the early and middle 1920's. I had left Oxford in 1924. He was to live for thirty-eight more years, and we were to see each other many times, but never for very long and never again with the day-by-day intimacy of brothers growing up together. Certain it is that few (and none of his contemporaries) ever gained greater renown in the field of literature, received more honors, or had more written about them than did Bill. As the only surviving member of our immediate family, these things, good and bad, I remember best about him.

His own character prevented him from being what one might call a happy man. His measure of life was not how long one could enjoy it, but what he did with it. Had he been given a choice between a long life without liquor or a short one with it, he would have immediately and without hesitation taken the latter, unfettered by apprehension and unconcerned with remorse. He would never pry into the affairs of others and insisted that others show him the same consideration. He felt that the ultimate in weak and worthless character was the man who would lie to advance his own cause or to save his own skin; on the other hand, one had no choice but to lie without hesitation to ease a mental or physical burden on one more feeble and unfortunate than himself.

He loved the South, especially Mississippi, and felt that the old days, meaning those before the War Between the States, were the best of all. Until the Supreme Court decision of 1954, which decreed that the Negroes must be made happy and that this could only be done by surrounding them with white people, we never talked about a "racial problem." Neither Bill nor any other member of our family ever voiced any anguish over the fact that some of our ancestors had held slaves. He believed, as we all did, that though the Negroes had been freed they were still our responsibility and always would be; an example of this was how he gladly and whole-heartedly looked after our Mammy Callie and an old family servant, Uncle Ned Barnett, long after their working days had ended. To Bill, this was a clear and inescapable obligation, and he would no more have shirked it than he would have let his own family go hungry.

I have read statements by some who professed to believe that Bill considered the white and black races to be equal. He never said anything in my presence to indicate any such con-viction. His compassion was great, but it did not include any feeling of sympathy for those who complained of their own lot and expected others to improve it for them.

He was not tall (about five feet six or seven inches), and what he said to me once, out of a clear sky so to speak, made me realize for the first time how his own lack of height affected him. We were talking about an FBI case I had in which I had participated in the arrests of several men, and I mentioned in passing that one had been a big, brawny ex-prizefighter. This led us to the subject of fighting, and I mentioned that every man and boy has to do some of it at one time or another. He replied that this certainly was the case, except that the little fellow had to do more of it because few will back off from him. However true this may be, certain it is that Bill never backed off from anyone.

Bill had a peculiar quirk in his character which caused him not only to belittle himself, but to raise no hand when others did it. I have in mind his repeated reference to himself as the world's oldest sixth-grader. True enough, his formal education did not extend far beyond that grade, which of course was little enough in itself, but if a man can be self-educated in a subject which interests him (literature, for instance) then few ever attained his level of competence.

When I was living in New Orleans in 1951, I received a call from him, and he told me that he would be there with Mother and his wife on a certain date to accept an award. I had noticed an article in a local paper which said that the French government was going to confer the Legion of Honor on him through its consul at New Orleans. My wife, being French, naturally wanted to make a good impression on the home folks, so she sent my extra suit to the cleaner, bought me a new tie, got out my best shirt, and even prodded me into having my shoes shined. On the date of the presentation we decked out in our finery and went downtown, picked up the folks, and drove out to the French consulate on St. Charles Avenue. Bill was wearing the same unpressed trousers, unshined shoes, and hunting coat with the leather-reinforced sleeve pads that he had worn the previous day. At the consulate, amid reporters and local citizens of note, he received the decoration from the hands of the consul. He gave his acceptance speech in flawless French.

My wife (as a woman and French, to boot) remarked on his attire, the while making a feeble comparison with my sharply creased trousers and gleaming footwear. I told her not to worry—that a man of Bill's renown and affluence was above reproach and could wear whatever suited him, whereas I, having attained neither, was properly spic and span as became a man who had to try to indicate by his appearance what he was unable to prove by his deeds.

When he received the Nobel Prize, there was much comment in the press that he had never before owned (or worn) evening clothes. I could not help but recall how much he liked to wear evening clothes and how well they became him when he wore his at school dances at the University. He liked to dress well, and he liked just as much not to dress well. He was perfectly content to wear whatever, to him, the occasion demanded.

His home was an antebellum one, the residence itself, the barn, and the back lot cabin all having been constructed by slave labor. It stands at the end of a gravel driveway amid many trees and well back from the secondary road by which it is reached. It was exactly the sort of place he wanted, though many repairs and additions had to be made over the years before it was made into the very desirable living place it became. There was a gate at the entrance to his property, and he tried to keep it closed to all except his family and friends. In addition, he had a "Posted—No Trespassing" sign nailed to it. People came to Oxford from all over to see him and his home. The gate and sign stopped some, but not all. I doubt if anything nettled him more than a carload of strangers suddenly appearing where the driveway ended beside his front porch.

Mother told me several times that she never heard Bill more vehement than when he was speaking of those people who invaded his privacy. He told me that one day, when he had been working with his horses during the hot afternoon, he was sitting down on the front porch with a cooling glass of iced tea in his hand and his dogs stretched out quietly at his feet. Without warning his calm meditation was shattered and the dogs were set to barking furiously by two sedans filled with people charging up his driveway, spewing gravel over his flowers, and making his horses run for cover. Neither car slackened speed until both arrived near the steps leading to the porch, where they were braked to screeching stops, one right behind the other.

On the rare occasions when the notion struck him, Bill enjoyed recounting to a member of the family an event that seemed worthy of mention, not necessarily important, but memorable for some reason or another. This was one such, and I remember how he looked as he told me about it—face stern and words harsh one moment, closely followed by a gentle smile and a delightful chuckle. I asked him what happened next—after the uninvited and unwelcome visitors had upset him. He replied that all the occupants of each car contrived to get their elbows on the windowsills of the sides of the cars facing him, then cupped their faces in their hands and stared silently at him as though he had two heads and twice as many horns.

He loved the outdoors and was probably never more contented than when hunting, fishing, or flying. With him an automobile was solely a means of transportation, to get him to some place too far to walk to. He had an old Ford touring car for years and made several trips to and from California in it with his family and a Negro driver. He later had a cloth-topped Jeep and after that a fiery red Rambler station wagon.

California held no fascination for him; he went there, he told me, simply because the movie people paid him more money than he could get elsewhere. Nor was he any more fascinated by the movies than by the state in which they were produced. They were a highly questionable form of entertainment as far as he was concerned and, with a few exceptions, he had no great esteem for the people involved in the industry. He always spoke in friendly terms of director Howard Hawkes, who was also a pilot; Clark Gable, who liked to hunt; and actress Ann Harding, whom he described as a fine woman and deserving of success.

I was stationed in El Paso at the time of one of his periodic forays to the movie capital when I received a call that he had been away from his fine suite of offices for days. He had evidenced no desire or inclination to return, and it was hoped that some member of the family might prevail upon him to do so. I knew what to expect and, based on past experience, had precious litle hope that I would be able to accomplish anything. But I couldn't refuse, so I took the next plane to Hollywood.

My guess had been right; all I could do was to lend Bill a friendly ear until he himself decided that he had drunk enough for the time being. With his houseboy at the wheel of the ancient Ford, we roamed the countryside. I'm sure that the endless miles of stucco homes and concrete streets appalled him and he supported the sight of them only with a faint hope that sooner or later we would find ourselves on a dusty country road that would remind him of Mississippi.

A day or so later, very early in the morning, he called me and abruptly announced that he was going back to the salt mines. He took a cold shower, shaved, ate a hearty breakfast, called for his car, and invited me to come along, as though I had just arrived in Hollywood that moment and he was going to show me the sights. We went straightaway to the land of make believe. His suite of offices on the second floor was sumptuous: wall-to-wall carpets, direct and indirect lighting, a tremendous desk, heavy leather chairs, a clerk, and two stenographers, none having been honored by his presence in two weeks or so.

By this time I was a little anxious to see what, if anything, he was called upon to do to earn his keep, which I doubted not was considerable. Whatever it was, I was favored with no glimpse of it. He took his seat at the large desk while his surprised but eager stenographers stood posed with pencils hovering over virgin notebooks. The news of his return must have spread wide and fast, for his co-laborers in the field of fantasy began to appear and to express their collective delight at seeing him back on the job again and looking so well. By the time these friendly felicitations had been bantered back and forth it was time for lunch at the restaurant on the lot. But now that he was once again safely back in the fold no one paid any more attention to him than they did to me; thus we were free to watch some of the movies being shot all over the lot.

It was interesting to watch the pretty folk emoting with such abandon, but flying was a lot more fun. This was shortly after I had obtained my pilot's license and I told Bill that if he would get us out to an airport I would rent a plane and take him for a ride. He must have figured there was no pressing reason for returning to his office (after all he had already been there once that day), and he agreed immediately. We drove to a nearby airport, and I was happy to see a familiar plane, a four-place Fairchild, on the flight line. I would not need much of a check ride to convince the owner that I could handle it.

A pilot of the air service "shot" two landings with me and said I was on my own. When I taxied back to the hangar, Bill was sitting on a bench in front of it smoking his pipe. I don't know what he was thinking about, but it was evidently not me or the Fairchild as he paid no attention when I held open the cabin door and called to him. I asked the pilot to go over and tell him I was waiting. He did, and Bill got to his feet at once and came out to the plane and got aboard.

I remember the airport was close to the ocean and within a few moments we were out over it. The boats on the water below interested Bill, and he talked about them, but apparently Hollywood interested him no more from the air than it did on the ground. In any event, he pointed out no landmarks nor appeared to search for any. At one point I knew that we must be reasonably near the Pacific Palisades, where he resided while working for the movie people. When I asked him whether he thought he could recognize his home from the air, he replied that he doubted it, since it was but one among thousands, and he had found it practically impossible to distinguish even when driving along the street right in front of it.

I was seldom in Mississippi during those years and do not know how Bill managed finally to shake the stardust of Hollywood from his unwilling feet and do his movie writing at home in Oxford. There are several versions of how it came about. One was that he was seen so rarely in his offices that no one missed him when he cleared out. Another was that his valiant employers assumed he was still living down the street at Pacific Palisades, which was a little difficult to check because he would not answer a telephone any more in California than in Mississippi.

He had a natural and sustained aversion to the telephone, anywhere, anytime, and under any conceivable circumstances. Knowing how he felt about the ubiquitous device, and having pretty much the same ideas myself, I would call him on the telephone (which existed solely in deference to his wife and daughter) only as a matter of urgent necessity or to keep from having to walk all the way down to his house. I recall but one time when he answered the phone himself, and the sound of his voice on the line so shocked me that I hung up before I could get my breath and identify myself. Radio and

television struck him with horror, too, and as far as I know
he never owned one or the other. The subject of the latter
came up during one of the last talks I had with him. He
mentioned that he had never watched one work and had no
intention of doing so. He laughed and said that he had noticed an article in a paper relating that some people in a
large eastern city who lacked TV sets would buy and erect
sprouts (as he termed the antennae) on their roofs so the
neighbors would assume the presence of a TV set beneath.
He concluded by saying that such desire and vanity were beyond his comprehension. Mine, too!

He loved horses and was fascinated by mules. I suppose,
as a general rule, a man would be hard put to find much to
say about a mule, but Bill not only mentioned them from
time to time in conversation but wrote some moving passages about the beasts. I think his feeling toward them was a
sort of compassion born of reflecting that a mule is actually
nothing more than a freak of nature, being neither born of
nor capable of giving birth to its own kind. He regarded animals in the same light as he did human beings: neither asked
to be here, both were, and both had to exist the best way they
could. But nature had discriminated against animals at the
outset by not providing them with voice or reason, and the
mule got the meanest and lowest break of all. Yet, to him,
they were worthy of the highest admiration as being the most
resolute of animals, always standing on their own four feet
and, in a real sense, eternally daring anyone to try to push
them off. This was a sentiment that Bill could appreciate,
admire, and never forget.

It was in keeping with his character that he kept none of
the honors that were bestowed on him—that is, in a physical
sense. All were taken to the museum at Oxford. I'm sure he
was justly proud of them all, but he was not the sort who had

to have daily reminders in front of him as evidence of what he had accomplished in life. As far as I know, he went to the museum only on rare occasions and then only to please some member of the family.

May his great soul have finally found the peace and tranquility in the hereafter that he kept himself from experiencing so often on earth.

About 3 A.M. on July 6, 1962, the telephone rang in our apartment at Mobile. It was my nephew Jimmy, and he told me that Bill had just died. I had not seen Bill since he drove me to the Oxford airport following Mother's funeral almost two years before. We had not then enjoyed the old affectionate companionship that had existed all our lives until the public stand taken by him in favor of school integration following the Supreme Court decision in 1954. The feelings of the rest of us were directly opposite to those sentiments expressed by him. We knew that he had only to speak to receive wide publicity, and we had no reason to think that his views on mixing the white and Negro races were not identical to our own. I doubt that Mother could ever bring herself to believe Bill actually meant what he publicly said. As for my own feelings, I can only say that I never knew him to say anything he didn't mean. On the other hand, he had Negro servants practically all his life, and I never heard him say anything to indicate that he wanted or expected the two races to associate otherwise.

It was not a pleasant subject to discuss with him after the 1954 decision, and I recall only one instance when we did discuss it, albeit briefly. We were en route to the airport after Mother's funeral, and I brought up the subject, feeling that perhaps it was long past due, by saying that I could not understand how he, whose life had been so much like my own, could have arrived at the conclusion he had expressed about integrating the schools. He replied that we needed to protect our image throughout the world and that I would eventually realize that his stand was the right one. I told him that such an assertion, coming from him of all people, was incomprehensible to me, since he was by nature so independent, stood so firmly on his own two feet, that he had never been known to give a tinker's damn what his next door neighbor thought of him, let alone to trouble himself one second over whether or not he or his country found approval in the eyes of other races in other lands. He made no reply.

But whatever our differences on this matter (we never had any other) he was still my big brother; I had always loved him and always would. I boarded the first plane for Oxford, and, as I flew over the land of our native state, my memory went back to the years of so long ago: sleeping as only tired and carefree children can sleep in our beds side by side; the new, exciting, and happy events which befell us day after contented day; the fine charges we made on our ponies to sweep the Yankees out of our beloved Southland; the quick and effortless adjustment of the active imagination of little boys in changing the back pasture to the broad, open prairies, where we would descend mightily on the ever-present, ever-roving bands of red men; the soft gentle days of enchanted springtime when, with Mammy Callie holding Dean in her arms, Bill, John, and I would go "bird nesting" in the far, exciting reaches of Bailey's Woods; the cold, grey, low-hanging clouds of early winter when we would all gather in Mammy's cabin and munch happily on hickory nuts and red and white sticks of peppermint candy while being enraptured by her endless tales of small animals and big wars.

And I thought of how much he had done for all of our people, a good portion of which I had not known until years after the events. When our father died in 1932, Bill considered himself as head of our clan, and so did we. It was a natural role for him, and he assumed it at once, without fanfare, but with dignity and purpose. He liked to have the family come to him with their troubles and problems, none being too great or small to favor with his undivided attention. I did not see him a great deal during those years, and, though I had my share of troubles in common with everyone else, they were too far away and, in a sense, too foreign for me to bother him with. But he never failed to try in his patient and reserved way to get me to share whatever problems I had with him.

When I got to Oxford the town was filled with reporters and photographers from all over the country. Some of them came to me expressing a hope of obtaining details of Bill's last days and of his funeral on the morrow. Arrangements were made for all of the newsmen to meet Jimmy and me at the dining room of a local restaurant that evening. Jimmy and I told them of his death; that he was in bed, was heard to suddenly gasp for breath, and then his heart stopped beating. We made no further reference to any details, but it has since been published that he had been drinking and had died after being admitted to a small hospital near Olive Branch, Mississippi.

During his lifetime Bill had made every effort to keep his estate inviolate; therefore we told the newsmen that we understood their mission and wished to cooperate with them, but that we could not permit them to make interviews or take photographs at his residence. We asked only that they handle their assignments with the understanding befitting the event. All agreed at once and, so far as I know, none violated the agreement.

Bill's ideas as to the disposition of his body after death were similar to those of Mother. He mentioned to me several times that he wanted to be put underground with as little delay and expense as possible. He was buried in a plot in the cemetery not far from where Mother, Father, and Dean rested and closer still to where John would be laid to his final rest before the coming of another summer.

The next day Jimmy came by the house, and I asked him to drive me to the Dean Falkner Memorial Airport, which was still operated by our friend "Champ" Champion and his son Dean Falkner Champion (now also a pilot-instructor). Having found in 1946 that I could not support an airplane and a wife too, I had sold my plane. I flew a rented plane a little in 1947, then gave it up completely, but always with the hope that finances would permit me to take it up again some day. This meant that I had not, in 1962, held the controls of an aircraft for more than fifteen years. Champ had a little Taylor Colt at the airport. It was equipped with a tricycle landing gear, and my flying had all been done in the days when such planes were few and far between; none I had ever flown had been so equipped.

We got the Colt out of the hangar and Dean said he would check me out in it. We taxied to the end of the runway, turned onto it, and I opened the throttle. We had scarcely begun to roll forward when the old love for flying flooded again upon me. It was as though I had last flown fifteen minutes or fifteen days, rather than fifteen years before. The old flying touch was still there, needing only an airplane upon which to exercise it. We shot two landings and performed a few maneuvers, and Dean said if we would return to the field, the plane was all mine to fly as I wished; that I had no need for anyone to cart me about the sky in a plane. I landed, Dean got out, and I took the plane up again—alone. It was, as always, wonderful beyond compare, satisfying beyond any want, and exhilarating beyond any sensation I have ever known. And I was sixty-three.

Then only John and I were left of the six in our immediate
family. He did not look well, and I asked him about his
health, especially whether the old, agonizing back pain still
persisted. His only comment was that he had lost some weight
(a glance had already told me that) but hoped to gain it back.

John was far and away the handsomest one of us all, and
his mind was in keeping with his personal appearance. I doubt
if Bill, with his remarkable brain, had an easier time in school
than John, who had considerably more of it, going on to ob-
tain an engineering degree from the University and lacking
only a few hours of getting a master's degree. I remember how,
as children, we would get together in the evenings after supper to prepare our lessons for the next day. Bill and John
would finish theirs before I could barely get started. I recall
no instance when either ever had to appeal to Mother for assistance, which was just as well, as she always had her hands
full with me.

As will happen to any boy sooner or later, he is going to
run across another who is ready and anxious to make a Christian endeavor to knock his teeth down his throat. There was
such a one in John's grade at grammar school and he had
licked the tar out of most of the boys in it, as well as several
in higher grades. John had as little aversion to battle as the
bully, so one afternoon they repaired to the area behind the
schoolhouse to "have it out." John was a little late getting
home that day; his shirt was torn, and he had a black eye which
would stay with him for several days. He made no remarks
about what had happened, and Bill and I put no questions to
him, but Mother did immediately. He got out of giving her
any details, but was less fortunate with Father later on.

We found out the next day that it had been one of the best
fights any of the excited and fascinated spectators had seen in
months and, if John showed a few marks, "You ought to see
the other fellow." John had, in fact, beaten the bully until

he had, for the first time in anyone's memory, said that he had
had enough.

John was blessed with an exceedingly retentive memory,
loved to talk (in this respect being almost totally different
from the rest of us), and was truly a walking encyclopedia on
the War Between the States. He shared Mother's talent for
painting, much of Bill's for storytelling, and, like Dean, had
one of the gentlest, surest touches on the controls of an airplane I ever saw. His humor was spontaneous and uproarious,
rather than whimsical and subtle as was Bill's. He was also
blessed, or cursed, with an almost insatiable optimism. I truly
believe that he could have smiled with hope and unalterable
faith had the world been tumbling down about him.

Beyond any doubt, this lifelong hope and faith rode with
him when he was taken to a Memphis hospital for a serious
emergency operation in March, 1963. He had undergone
many of them during the preceding twenty years. This one
would be the last. His son Jimmy called me from the hospital,
and I proceeded there by the first plane from Mobile. He was
under care to build up his system for an operation the following week. I talked to his doctors, and they expressed confi-
dence that he would be able to stand the operation and make
a good recovery thereafter. I remained at the hospital two
days and talked to John several times. Even in the hospital
bed his close cropped, iron-grey hair and sky-blue eyes set off
his fine, regular features. He told me that he was certain he
could be up and about within a short time after the operation. I had just bought a new home in Mobile, and he promised to come with his wife Lucille to visit us as soon as he
could travel. When I went in to say good-by I put my hand
on his head, and he gently patted my other hand resting on
the side of the bed and again assured me that everything was
going to be all right and that he would soon see me in Mobile.
I turned and left, never to see him again.

Jimmy kept in touch with me by long distance and on the eve of the operation said that John was in good humor and that the doctors expressed no apprehension concerning the approaching operation. The next day, about noon, Jimmy called again; the aftermath of the operation had not gone well, and John was much weaker than the doctors had predicted. I told Jimmy that I would go to the airport at once and get aboard a plane due out for Memphis within two hours. At the airport I hurriedly bought a ticket from a clerk in the ticket office with whom I was acquainted. I got aboard the Memphis plane, the door was closed, and the plane started to taxi away from the ramp. We had gone but a short distance when the plane suddenly stopped, and I could hear the entry door being opened again. Someone ran up the aisle and touched me on the shoulder. It was the ticket clerk, and he said, "Mr. Falkner, the family called and said to tell you not to go on to Memphis, but to get off at Oxford. Your brother is dead."

John was dead. Now I alone was left, the last of the four Falkners. We flew northward and soon the familiar terrain of Mississippi was passing steadily beneath the plane, and memories of so many things of so many years past rushed upon me; of Father and Mother, Bill, John, Dean, and Mammy Callie about the fireside in the living room, the lives of all so closely interwoven that it seemed as though the lives of all would go on forever.